Lakshmi Purana

Lakshmi Purana

Balaram Das

Translated by
Lipipuspa Nayak

Black Eagle Books
2021

Black Eagle Books
USA address:
7464 Wisdom Lane
Dublin, OH 43016

India address:
E/312, Trident Galaxy, Kalinga Nagar,
Bhubaneswar-751003, Odisha, India

E-mail: info@blackeaglebooks.org
Website: www.blackeaglebooks.org

First International Edition Published by
Black Eagle Books, 2021

LAKSHMI PURANA
by **Balaram Das**
Translated by **Lipipuspa Nayak**

Translation Copyright © Lipipuspa Nayak

All rights reserved. No part of this publication may be reproduced, stored in a retrieval system, or transmitted, in any form or by any means, electronic, mechanical, photocopying, recording or otherwise without the prior permission of the publisher.

Cover & Interior Design: Ezy's Publication

ISBN- 978-1-64560-231-6 (Paperback)
Library of Congress Control Number: 2021951471

Printed in the United States of America

FOREWORD
Hrusikesh Panda

ONE

Lakshmi Purana is a paean to goddess Lakshmi, the goddess of wealth and prosperity. Lakshmi is the wife of Vishnu, one of the trinity of Sanatan or Hindu religion. Vishnu has been progressively identified with Brahmam, the all-pervading consciousness of universe, omnipresent and omniscient, and who has no beginning and no end. He has to appear in mortal earth, as avatar or incarnation, for a cause when Dharma or righteousness is subdued and overtaken by absence of dharma. Vishnu is worshipped in the earth in simple human forms, sometimes in the forms of his incarnations. Puri is the abode of Jagannatha (the form of Vishnu), his elder brother Balabhadra and sister Subhadra. They are worshipped together on a throne in the sanctum sanctorum of the main temple. Lakshmi is worshipped in another temple next to the main temple.

The four Vedas, first in a spoken medium and later in written language, are the earliest sacred scriptures of

Hinduism. In fact, these are the first texts in any language in the world, to have a script, and a script arranged with scientifically phonetic order capturing all the sounds of human beings across the world. The first Veda, Rig Veda is the earliest among the scriptures. By sixth century CE, many kings in India had become Buddhists, though the population at large remained Hindu. Shankara, an itinerant scholar of the Vedas and Upanishads and other scriptures of Hindu dharma went around the country to establish Hindu heritage and identified Puri as the site of Rig Veda. According to the records kept at Kalady, birthplace of Shankara, he had identified the Vedic *kshetras* (*peetha or peethams*) as Puri of Rig Veda, Dwaraka of Sama Veda, Shringeri of Yajur Veda, and Jyotirpeetha of Atharva Veda.

Shankaracharya is believed to have finished his task at the age of 32, and established four hermitages at Govardhan peetha in Puri, Shringeri peetha in Karnataka, Sharada peetha at Dwaraka in Gujarat, and Jyotirpeeth in Uttarakhand. He is believed to have lived in seventh century CE. His main concern was to understand the spiritual and eternal value of Veda, and his main discourses are about Brahmasutra, Upanishad and Shrimad Bhagavat Gita. They are about the universal and eternal meaning of existence beyond the rituals of Veda; but he also identified many places of significance for Sanatan dharma for the benefit of everyone. He left his mortal body at Kedaranath at the age of 32. When Shankar appeared, many households of kings were under the sway of Jainism and Buddhism. This undermined the understanding, the spiritualism and the knowledge (in astronomy, in Ayurveda and in aesthetics and language) of Sanatan Dharma. Another practice of Buddhism and Jainism of not working for four months in a year during rainy season was destructive of the economy and encouraged idle people to escape the duties of four phases of life envisaged under Sanatan Dharma.

The present temple of god Jagannath (at Puri) was built in 12th century. Before this, there was another temple which is found in the sparse records of the construction of 12th Century CE. Odisha, which was also known as Kalinga in the *Mahabharata* and Udra in earlier references, was a maritime country and the temple of Jagannath also was a landmark for the sea-faring ships. The seafarers were known as *Sadhaba*s, meaning honest persons. In 7th or 8th century CE, when Shankar visited Puri the older temple existed.

According to the history of Puri *peetha*, this has existed since 483 BCE – a date arrived at through the calculation of movement of the solar plane in the universe; this is explained briefly in the footnotes.[1]

---

[1] Indian astronomy had recognized in Vedic times, that while the planets in solar system revolved around the Sun, the whole solar system was also moving in the space where stars moved. (Where astronomers and astrologers believed that earth was still and Sun and other planets moved around earth, it did not affect the astronomical chart which measured the angular separation between different bodies; the results were not different as long as the accuracy of celestial bodies' position was comparable.) The different position in astronomical chart when movement of solar plane was recognised was known as *Ayanamsha*. For this purpose, a really far off star is invariably in a far off galaxy. The dimensions were like this: the diameter of solar plane is about one billion kilometers, a star in Sagittarius (Dhanu) galaxy which had been referred to as a stable star was ten thousand light years away, and the dimension of the universe is unknown but may be around ten billion light years away. Irrespective of whether you believe in astrology or not, any Indian astrologer can say whether the ayanamsha or correction necessary because of movement of solar plane, has been corrected and this correction is called ayanamsha correction, and a corrected horoscope is called nirayana based one. The difference in location of stellar bodies due to ayanamsha was about 0 degree 0 minute and less than a second per year. It also depended on which distant star the ayanamsha calculation was based. This was ayanamsha correction, and was started around 2500

Before the Shankar of seventh century CE, Adi Shankar had been born who had established these four peethas (Shankar re-established these keeping the emergence of other religions and certain amount of decline in Hindu religion). He was born when Vedic religion was giving way to easier forms like rituals, and seers held that the core meaning of mantras in Veda was about Yajna. Adi Shankar re-established the spiritual and cosmic importance of Veda as the prime one, while the ritualistic aspects were meant for people who could not achieve the prime goal. The other Peethas give the year of establishment as 491 BCE (Dwaraka), 483 BCE (Sringeri) and 485 BCE (Jyotirmath). The analysis about the determination of time shows that these different years actually refer to one or two years around 490 BCE. The core mantra of Shankar's ashrams was *Prajnanam Brahmam*: the consciousness that the atman is a part of the universal Brahmam.

Purana was one form of sacred texts which provided easier access to achieving religious goal. There were originally eighteen Purana(s) written in Sanskrit and rendered to other Indian languages over years and centuries. *Lakshmi Purana* was not one of them. It was composed in early part of 16th century CE in Odia and had unusual concerns. But it became a sacred Purana recited at homes and Bhagavat Ghara on every Thursday. *Bhagabata* recreated by Jagannath Das at the same time from *Bhagavat Purana* was the other sacred text which was recited every day in the houses of Odisha.

BCE in India. So if a correct astrological or astronomical chart is available of a past occurrence, year of occurrence can be derived. The ancient four peethas were set up during the last decade of 5th Century BCE. This is not hagiography, as some Wikipedia contributors claim.

TWO

Natyashastram by Bharatamuni was written in 5th century BCE.[2] This treatise is about principles of performing arts and in course of it, is a documentation and chronicle of Indian languages. Odia language, like many Indian languages, was derived from Sanskrit. Odisha was variously known as Kalinga, Utkal, Koshal and Udra at different times and for various geographical regions of the state. There was, and is, a large population of forest dwellers and the thick forests of Odisha kept its culture somewhat distinct. Odia or Udra language became distant from Sanskrit as the local words were included in the language and their spoken oral traditions also influenced the way Udra language was spoken.[3] Sabara was and is a major forest-dwelling community of Odisha. This community, with various changes in spellings like Sa'ara, Saura, Suara, Saora had a distinct language known as *Shabarabhasha* and *Shabari* in *Natyashastram*.[4] In drama, such languages were to be assigned to charcoal-makers, hunters, gatherers of forest produce, and for keepers of large herds of domestic animals like horses and elephants. Udra language was assigned to characters like finders and diggers of subterranean passages, prison warders, horse-riders and heroes who are trying to escape.[5]

---

[2] *Natyashastram* has been cited to be of 2nd century BCE (and not earlier) for the sole reason that it carries the word 'shraman'. However, 'shraman' is a Sanskrit word and also applied to Jain monks who were common in 5th century BCE. Also 'shraman' is seen in Panini's Sutrapada '*kumar shramanadivih*' (2.1.70).

[3] *Natyashastram* of Bharatmuni (18.48)

[4] *Natyashastram*, 18.53

[5] *Natyashastram*, 18.54

This shows that the language of Odisha was not as close to Sanskrit as it should have been. The society also did not follow a caste system rigidly.

There are many opinions to explain the origin of god Jagannath in Puri. Almost all of them have one aspect in common: the deities were worshipped by Sabara people in a deep forest and the king of Puri worshipped for years and requested the Sabara king that the god be installed in Puri. This could have been dismissed as one of the 'myths' except for the fact that the successors of the Sabara people cook the offerings before the gods which is bought by the devotees. The Prasad is called Mahaprasad. *Maha* and *bada* or great are epithets used in Jagannatha temple for many things such as Mahodadhi (the sea), Mahadipa (the lamp atop the temple), Badadeula (the temple), Badadanda (the road on which chariots are drawn). 'Suara' is a spoken version of Sabara, as per the principles documented in *Natyashastram*, where consonants are replaced by vowels, the vowel 'a' is replaced by 'aa' and so on. The Record-of-Rights of the temple distinguishes between different categories of Suara. Suara badu sprinkles the path from the kitchen to the abode of the deities and takes the first offering of prasadam to the deities. Suara and mahasuara prepare the prasadam. The Suara are divided into several categories[6]: bada, pitha, tuna, thali, amalu, bindalu, amalu, toil, pagua, dola badu, dola bati and others.

In *Lakshmi Purana*, when Lakshmi is asked to go away by Jagannatha and Balabhadra, she says in reply: 'Because

---

[6]Report of the Special Officer, Puri Shri Jagannath Temple Administration Act, 1952 for 1954, published in Orissa Gazette dated January 12, 1955.

you are great people, your misdeeds are not known to the world…you brothers are crazy for Sabara people. Why do you forget this?'[7]

THREE

The absence of caste system as rigid as in North-west and the language which was not as pure made Kalinga a somewhat lesser country than the North-western parts of India. The *Shatapath Brahman* ordained: 'Since the Arya people of eastern part of Bharat have followed a new path ignoring Vedic dharma and rituals, since the social customs of areas like Koshal are different from Kuru and Panchal, since these eastern Indians do not recognize Brahmins as the authority over the social system, and since they cannot pronounce Sanskrit in its purest form as their language has been corrupted by other languages, the people of Brahmabarta should not go to these places.'[8]

These observations were not surprising in the context of what has been said earlier about Udra developing as a somewhat independent and inclusive civilization. For most of centuries, Kalinga remained a rich and militarily dominant kingdom. When Ashoka invaded Kalinga, in his stone edict he declared the number of people killed at figures which exceed the total number killed in the two world wars. He went upto Jaugad in Ganjam district and declared that this was the last point of Kalinga empire and he had thus vanquished the entire Kalinga empire. Kalinga empire extended beyond Vijayanagaram and parts of Vishakhapattanam, some 500 kilometres away as evidenced

---
[7]Lakshmi Purana, canto 194-196.

[8] Prof Benimadhab Padhi, *Darudevata*, 1964, where he has translated this excerpt from *Shatapath Brahman* into Odia. Included in *Benimadhab Granthabali*, Friends Publishers, Cuttack, 2019.

by Kalinga style temples in the area. And if indeed so many people of Kalinga were killed, how did this country raise an army a generation later, vanquish Magadh and regained the holy relics stolen by Ashoka? In the *Mahabharata* war, Kalinga soldiers participated on the side of Kauravas[9]. The king of Utkal had been invited to Rajasuya Yajna of Yuddhisthir[10], the eldest Pandava brother. Kalinga and Utkal kingdoms were thus not in favour of either Kauravas or Pandavas and were independent. During Muslim invasion in the north and south of Kalinga, it remained a Hindu kingdom, unaffected by alien culture. Muslim invaders attacked and looted Puri temple 18 times with limited success between 1540 to 1690, but that happened after *Lakshmi Purana* was written. These facts are not surprising.

But what is surprising is the composition of *Lakshmi Purana* by Balaram Das in the early part of 16th century. The forest-dwellers had sacred functions in the temple. The caste discrimination in society was so low that puritans had declared the place as unfit for visit by Vedic Arya people. There is no record that people of any caste were prohibited from entering the temple. Balaram Das, himself had little to complaint; though he was not born a Brahmin, he was of a fairly upper caste and his father worked as an officer in the king's court.

The theme of the *Purana* is that, goddess Lakshmi visits the houses of people on sacred days who keep their houses clean and follow rituals and she bestows her blessings and gifts on them. She does not distinguish on the basis of caste. One of her favourite devotees is Shriya (which is another name of Lakshmi), and one Thursday in

---

[9]*Mahabharata*, Bhishma Parba.

[10]*Mahabharata*, Sabha Parba, 31. 71-72.

Margashira month, when she finds this woman of *chandaal* caste clean, and pious, she gives her blessings on the spot and Shriya becomes rich with wealth of cattle, land, gold, gemstones, a palatial house, a family of sons and promises that Shriya will go to heaven after her death. What Lakshmi finds are somewhat prejudiced against the well off – the house of a Sadhaba, a sea-faring trader is disorderly and the lady of the house has not even heard of the sacred day. Lakshmi educates the women not only the sacred needs of worshipping the goddess, she also tells them about the duties of the women to their houses and families.

Her visits are irksome to god Balabhadra who has seen the conduct of his brother's wife through his divine eyes. (For some reason the writer has said that Jagannath and Balabhadra were returning from a hunting in the forest, another unusual remark which needs some examination.) When Lakshmi returns from her visit to the temple, she is asked to go away by Jagannath on the insistence of Balabhadra. Lakshmi leaves with a curse that the two brothers will not get rice to eat, water to drink or clothes to wear for twelve years until they come begging to her.

During the argument between Jagannath and Lakshmi, she reminds him that at their wedding, when he lost in the game of cowries, he had granted her wish that she will mingle with the poorest forms of life, including destitute lives. She reminds him that while he had gone and taken food with people of all descriptions, and taken shelter in their houses, he is holding it as an unpardonable crime that Lakshmi stood near the entrances of the houses of some people who are kept at a distance (*Lakshmi Purana*, canto 186-198). When she engages others to fulfil her curse, she says that unless she does this, in Kaliyuga men will not look for their wives (*LP*, cantos 239-241). When god Jagannath and his brother finally beg for food from Lakshmi, without knowing that this was her house but of a *chandaal*, she is satisfied that her curse has been fruitful (*LP*, canto 460-485)[11]. Yet before this happened, the brothers wanted to cook food with the provisions supplied by her because cooked food from her house was untouchable. She supplied the provisions but requested Agni, the god of fire, that the fuelwood shall not burn, because if men started to cook they will not care for women in future (*LP*, canto 361-374).

Earlier Lakshmi has advised what is appropriate for a happy and stable life. A woman should not ignore the pious attitude necessary for her worship. At the same time, she should not ignore her husband. Women who ignore their household, have affairs outside marriage or roam around outside without purpose will suffer. (*LP*, canto 92-96). Those women who leave the house and engage themselves in unnecessary rituals also suffer (*LP*, canto 108). She also prescribes mores for men. These and subsequent assertions suggest that while caste based and otherwise disorder had not happened at the time of this incident, this may happen in future and the actions of goddess Lakshmi are to protect the future order. Yet she puts some conditions for return to the temple: that in the temple, Brahmins and *chandaals* will share food. Goddess Lakshmi intends to put a clean and stable social order in place with words, rewards and punishments. The social order was primarily with respect

---

[11] These deviations appear to have been set by the earlier practice of Buddhists to abandon work, roam around and live off others. This also appears to have been directed towards the influx of easy Vaishnavism where men and women left their duties to perform samkirtan in the streets. Chaitanya had come to Puri round this time.

to the rights and equality of the women, the weak, and the poor, in the present and in the future.

Four

For her husband, however, Lakshmi follows more arduous and painful paths for the same reason. God Jagannath with all the divinity, who created the universe and ran the universe could not escape the curse. In order to fulfil the curse, she takes the help of Vishwakarma (the builder/architect for gods), the Betalas (strongmen of gods), Nidravati (goddess of sleep), Saraswati (goddess of wisdom), Agni (god of fire), Vayu (god of air) and so on. Jagannath, however, quietly suffers the pain and deprivation cast upon him as a curse, and machinated by Lakshmi actively. God Shri Krishna says in Gita: 'In the three worlds, I have no duty cast upon me, to perform karma. I have nothing to get from this world. Yet, I am always engaged in karma.'[12]

Jagannatha is Brahmam, and is not subject to Prakriti, to the extent of being compelled to perform karma. Krishna says: 'If I do not perform karma, then the universe will be devastated, and I will be the cause of total disorder and all destructions.'[13]

Goddess Lakshmi, however, is performing her karma through Prakriti. Krishna says: 'Even the wise people work under Prakriti in such manner as their nature and wisdom decide. In this creation, every living being is bound to perform karma under the control of Prakriti.[14] Jagannath as

---

[12]Bhagavad Gita, 4.22.

[13]Bhagavad Gita 2.24

[14]Bhagavad Gita 2'33

Purushottama, the ultimate Purusha, does not obstruct the path of Lakshmi[15]. The creator of the Universe has created eternal laws which govern the creation. He cannot break the laws that govern the universe, as this will lead to chaos. That is why Krishna convinces Arjuna to take arms in the war of Dharma, the *Mahabharata* war. That is why Lakshmi performs the karma to protect a just social order, and not Jagannatha.

Five

The period when Odia *Bhagabata* and *Lakshmi Purana* were written, has been described by many historians as the end of glorious period of Kalinga. Since fifth century BCE until 1500 CE Kalinga (most of present day Odisha) was an untrammelled military and economic power. The political equation of India had been changing and Muslims had been invading and establishing garrisons in many parts of India. Hindu population was massacred in many places; but Hindu kings also defended their territories fiercely. Kalinga was never under any real control of Muslim invaders. When Akbar's (16th CE) army came to the northern border of Kalinga, they faced such disasters and death that their General Mansingh said: 'This country cannot be defeated; it is the land of God Jagannath.' But the kings of Kalinga had been wasting too much energy on wars with Hindu kings of South instead of protecting the Northern border.

One aspect of Kalinga administration was the large number of feudatory states having nominal or financial subordination; it was not a monolithic government. After 1500 CE, the kings settled back to the normal governance. Another aspect of Kalinga governance, was that while they

---

[15]Bhagavad Gita 15.18

maintained a small regular army, most people who fought during wars were people who were farmers, artisans, painters and artists. After the wars they returned to their normal avocations. The end of the wars gave full and free opportunity to the artists, including writers and performing artists. Among the major compositions of the period are the *Bhagabata* by Jagannath Das, *Ramayana* by Balaram Das, a number of mystical compositions, doomsday predictions, and Puranas derived from the original eighteen Sanskrit Puranas. However *Bhagabata* was the only religious text which was sung aloud in villages in the community religious houses, where Krishna was worshipped often in the form of *salagram*. In addition, *Lakshmi Purana* was recited on Thursdays in either individual houses or community houses. Jagannath Das steered clear of Radha as she was never a presence in the Sanskrit *Bhagavata Purana*. A new trend of poetry centred around Radha. Radha as a concert of Krishna had been mentioned in one Purana and there is a word Radha in Shankar's *Jagannatha Ashtakam*. However *Geeta Govinda,* based on the theme of Radha and Krishna, by Jayadev, composed at Puri in 12th century CE became popular as it was recited in many temples of Odisha, accompanied Odissi dance and the poetic value of Radha theme dominated several parts of Odisha in musical pieces and Odissi songs.

There were several forms of performing arts across Odisha such as pala, daskathia, suanga, dadhi, jatra, gitinatya, and katha (such as *Nala-Damayanti katha*) which were played in day or night, which carried narratives in different styles to the accompaniment of local musical instruments. There was a vast surge of lyrical poetry which was written or revived giving to generations of *chautisha, koili* songs, *champu, chhanda, odissi,* and *kaandana* (wedding songs). Among the performing arts of forest dwellers, 'sabara-sabaruni', 'chandaala-chandaaluni', 'chadheia-chadheiani' are some names which they go by, although many songs have different names within the respective communities. Several genres of devotional songs were also popular such as janana, stuti, sarpa janana, bhajana, and prarthana. The *Mahabharata* by Sarala Das was composed in the 15 century CE, and it was extensively inspirational and in many ways different from the original Sanskrit text, unlike *Bhagabata* of Jagannath Das which was composed in a language which continues to be the standard Odia language today.

Six

How did the mighty Kalinga empire fare? It did not disintegrate. The Afghan looters and invaders attacked Odisha from the unprotected north frontiers, destroyed temples between Balasore and Cuttack districts, looted and destroyed the spaces. In 1568, the last independent king of Odisha fought in person against the Afghans in Bhadrak district and was killed. Between 1568 and 1575, the Afghans looted various places in Odisha, stayed at a fort in Cuttack constructed by Hindu kings a thousand years ago, and did not play any other role in governance. The Muslim rulers collected religious tax or *jijiya* from the pilgrims of Car Festival (of Puri), but this did not last long. In 1575, a Mughal general attacked the Afghans and drove them out. But they did not try to govern Odisha, as their general said famously that Odisha is not to be defeated as this is the land of Jagannatha. They made the King of Khordha also the king of Puri, and vested the administration in their hands. From 1756 to 1803 Odisha came under the rule of Marathas, who also remained absentee rulers and left the governance to the local kings led by king of Puri. Marathas came before the Muslims could even change the name of the fort. Southern Odisha, had been gifted to the English by the Subedar of Hyderabad in 1762. But the king of Ghumsur did not know this, and refused to be subjugated, The British also went neck-deep in the day-to-day management of Ghumsur. The citizens, most of whom were forest dwellers, were extremely loyal to the Ghumsur dynasty. The Muslim ruler had successfully changed the name of the port at Rushikulya mouth to Ganj-e-aam, the granary, which became Ganjam. Anyway, the fooling around with Kandha (and Sabara tribes to a smaller number) and Ghumsur kingdom caused the forest dwellers to rise to a revolt lasting 60 years. So when the British came from Calcutta to occupy Odisha, they had no apparent resistance; but a debilitating war with the Hindu dispensation which continued to administer Odisha lasting 50 years reminded the British of their bitter experience in South Odisha. Their experience in Western Odisha was similar. So, they decided to leave the large number of Hindu kings ruling in the forest areas with a lot of independence. The British looked after the administration of four coastal districts only. They had also tried to run the Jagannatha temple; but after a couple of years restored this to the king of Puri. Some suggestions by successor British officers to annex these states (like Ravenshaw) were shut down by saner and more experienced people.

Seven

The translation of *Lakshmi Purana* is a formidable task. The language is often colloquial in today's standards. The foods are a formidable category by themselves. One had to know the ingredients that do not have even an approximate English equivalent; on top of that one had to know the elemental part of cooking! This is the kind of work which needs sponsoring by an institution; but the translator has done an excellent job all by herself.

Amidst this rich array of literary and devotional compositions, *Lakshmi Purana* continued to be recited in our house every Thursday. On some days it was my turn. There were some pronouns and verbs which were disrespectful, like when goddess Lakshmi was addresses as *tu* by her husband or his brother; in those lines I changed the pronoun to *tum* or *aap* with appropriate change in verbs as I recited. When the narration of Jagannath and Balabhadra suffering with hunger and Lakshmi conniving to perpetuate their suffering, a few drops of tear fell from eyes; after all I did not know the way gods' world worked. Neither do I know it now.

Hrusikesh Panda is a well-known writer of Odisha and has published eight novels, over 100 short stories, four plays and some literary essays. His novel *Garba Karibara Katha* (2010) is a researched work of Odisha's economy and society between 1400 to 1900 CE. He has a Master's degree in Chemistry, a Ph D in literature and MBA in Finance. He was the topper of 1979 batch of Indian Administrative Service and retired as a Secretary to Government of India.

Hrusikesh has made about a dozen films, for which he has composed the lyrics and music.

Translator's Note

Puri, a seacoast town of Odisha is the abode of Lord Jagannath, His elder bother Balabhadra (Balaram) and His sister Subhadra. Jagannath is an incarnation of Vishnu and was worshipped by the primitive people. According to one myth, Jara Sabara, a primitive hunter had killed Lord Krishna by mistake and repented. Krishna was an incarnation of Vishnu who had been born to remove injustice and impropriety and had ordained his own death at the hands of Jara; but Jara was a mere human being and did not know this. When Jara repented inconsolably, Krishna agreed to appear as Jagannath.

This myth signifies two realities: a) Puri was famous long before the Vaishnavite movement of 9th-10th century in South India, and b) the temple and rituals of Lord Jagannath remained impervious to the subsequent discrimination of people on the basis of 'caste' in other religious establishments.

Adi Shankaracharya born in present-day Kerala established four peethams to identify four important holy places for Hindus. These places represented four Vedas. Puri was named by Adi Shankaracharya as Govardhan Peetham and stood for Rig-veda. Sharada Peetham at Shringeri (Karnataka) stood for Yajur-veda. Dwaraka(Gujarat) represented Soma-veda and Jyotirmatha

(Uttaranchal) represented Atharva-veda. The chronicles of these peethams establish that Adi Shankaracharya was born in 509 B.C. and died in 477 B.C. at the age of 32. Rig Veda did not recognize division of human beings on the basis of birth – the basis that has generated the concept of class (and caste) with the advancement of civilization. The 'mantra' for Govardhan Peetham is 'Prajnanam Brahma' – 'The Universal Being is Knowledge'. A human being is assigned a place in the world order on the basis of his knowledge of the Universal Being. I am mentioning this fact here not to stake a parochial claim about the ancientness of Puri or pre-eminence of Lord Jagannath. The intention is purely literary: these facts provide some reason as to how the institution of Lord Jagannath managed by Hindus transcended the subsequent class barriers, and provide a background to understand the present text *Lakshmi Purana*.

With time Buddhists had claimed rights over the Jagannath temple at Puri. This fact suggests that the Deity was already worshipped by the time of invasion of Kalinga (much of the present day Odisha) by Ashoka (3rd century B.C.), who later became a Buddhist. The rise of Buddhism and Jainism with state patronage began to cause concern among Hindus. Shankaracharya (as distinct from Adi Shankaracharya), who was born in 686 AD. in South India, started another march following in the footsteps of his eponymous predecessor and re-established the Hindu order. He visited Puri. This was before the revival of Vaishnavism in South India. At least one earlier structure of a temple of Jagannath dating about 9th century A.D. has been proven through archaeological evidence. The present temple at Puri was built over the earlier structure around 12th century AD. This was also the time when poet Jayadev of Odisha wrote *Geetagovinda*, the masterpiece on the Radha-Krishna mystical lore, and verses from the text were sung in the temple.

There should be no doubt that these were conscious schemes. The revival of Vaishnavism in South India, the construction of the temple and its elaborate rituals for worshipping the deities must have been part of a Hindu missionary activity against the imminent fear of conversion of Hindus to Muslims. This fear was generated following the advent of the Sufis from Middle East Asia, who were converting Hindus to Muslims through preaching, instead of violence. The movement of Shankaracharya and Acharya Ramanuja (from South India) too was part of countering this proselytizing activism. Meanwhile, Kashmir, which produced the major storyteller of the world – Gunadhya (pre-Buddha) – was systematically converted to Muslim religion through the persuasive Sufists. This was wearisome for everyone. Vaishnavism began to simplify Hindu religion; from complex concepts it got down to simple story-telling.

Fast forward: Odisha. 12th century A.D. *Geetagovinda* of Jayadev establishes that the temple of Lord Jagannath at Puri was building up a culture of tolerance and ease in rituals. This lyrical and musical work must be remembered as a major Sanskrit text, which was not exactly religious, nor written in the shadow of any ancient Sanskrit text. Already, Puri as distinct from the other three primordial sanctuaries of Hindu religion, was becoming famous, particularly because it had done away with caste restrictions. Today, the largest volume of tourists in India goes to Titrupati, in Andhra Pradesh, and the second largest to Puri.

So, the identification of Lord Jagannath with Buddha is ancient. At least dated to the 'timing' of invasion of Kalinga set by the historians. The identification of Lord

Jagannath with Krishna, an incarnation of Vishnu, was complete by the time of the anointment of Puri as a Hindu spiritual quartet by Adi Shankaracharya. The Sanskrit of *Geetagovinda* is very close to Odia language. The subsequent major text in Odia language is *Bhagabata* by Jagannath Das (16th C). Jagannath Das wrote it in a recitable form as, in a sense, Jayadev had attempted. Jayadev wrote in a more classical format, which is the foundation of classical Odissi song and dance. The Odia in *Bhagavata* continues to be the standard Odia language.

By this time Balaram Das was composing *Lakshmi Purana*. There was some folklore on why Jagannath temple allowed all Hindus, including those who ate meat. The text is a scripturization of this rationale that reinforces the practice of admitting meat-eating Hindus to the temple. Balaram Das did not invent a scripture in the local tradition to allow the prohibited to enter the temple. His contribution to the lowering of barrier of caste antagonism can be decimated.

II

Balaram Das was born in the last part of 15th century He was one of the five great poets of Odisha during the 16th century who translated and reinterpreted some Sanskrit texts and also wrote original texts borrowing from local folklore, beliefs and mores. His father was a courtier in the court of Pratap Rudra Deb, the king under whom Odisha lost its political areas and strength as a warrior state. But the martial failure of the period also coincided with the buildup of standard Odia language and Odia literature away from the tyranny and snobbery of Sanskrit. The Sanskrit literature composed by writers of Odisha (from Jayadev to Bishwanath Kaviraj among others) was simpler, and to that extent was much less tyrannical. Odia literature gained patronage from a king, evolved to acquire a permanent identity and sustained itself through popular demand.

In one of his works, *Chhatish Gupta Gita* (thirty-six secret songs), Balaram Das has been categorical about his parentage, with mention of Somanath Mohapatra – a courtier of some influence at the court of Pratap Rudra Deb – being his father. A few other works of Balaram Das too carry this reference. Desiring immortality through works is a medieval phenomenon in Indian literary history, as classical Indian writers are known to have preferred anonymity. And by opting to put the record of his origin straight for history, Balaram may have trodden a nascent and innocuous practice. At another level, however, this helps to put in perspective the anxieties and riddles reigning the issues of social rank as well as creativity of these writers.

Balaram Das lived during the reign of Pratap Rudra Deb (1504-32), who lost his battle in the South of the country, became weak and probably fell back to the option of religion, in particular, the religious mood of Vaishnavism of the period. Vaishnavism – the religious cult that believes in the supremacy of Vishnu – in Odisha can be traced decisively to the arrival of Shankaracharya who canonized that Jagannath was a form of Vishnu. Krishna as an incarnation of Vishnu was also canonized, inter alia, the composition of *Geetagovinda*. This 12th century devotional song identified Jagannath with Krishna, who was a temporal incarnation of Lord Vishnu. Vaishnavism in Odisha had also been influenced by the devotional doctrine of 'Rama-bhakti' of Acharya Ramanuja. However, Rama as an incarnation of Vishnu had limited followers in Odisha until recently. Vaishnavism in Odisha was independent of Chaitanya Deb of Bengal. His arrival at Puri and submission before Lord Jagannath was one subsequent phase of this movement.

In some of his works Balaram refers to himself as a *shudra*. The word stands for one from the lowest class (caste) of Hindu society. Balaram Das probably meant that he was a non-Brahmin, and one from the caste of cultivators. 'Mohapatra', the epithet that he uses for his father, is a title, and not a surname. Balaram Das was not an untouchable by caste or class because his father held an important position in the king's court. The five poets had been inspired by non-casteism of the temple of Jagannath and reinterpreted the earlier scriptures. *Lakshmi Purana* is almost the epitome of this anti-caste, anti-class egalitarian philosophy of the new poets.

III

Lakshmi Purana, as the title explains, is the story of goddess Lakshmi in simple narrative verses. It is recited in every household of Odisha in the Hindu month of Margashira on all the four Thursdays. In most households, this text is recited throughout the year, every Thursday.

As a creative piece of work, the text stands on its own aesthetic as well as sociological strength. The text draws on the myths and folklore of the Jagannath temple of Puri and has no correspondence in the Sanskrit Puranic tradition. Besides its manifestly feminist orientation, the text also carries a brief against human evils such as untouchability and arrogance of the upper class.

Set in Puri, and the temple of lord Jagannath, the plot of the text spins around Lord Jagannath and Goddess Lakshmi. Yet, essentially *Lakshmi Purana* is a text with primacy for women casts. It is the story of Goddess Lakshmi:

the story of her disturbed domesticity, occasioned in the class-prejudice of her arrogant brother-in-law, her ridicule by her husband and brother-in-law and her consequent revenge at restoring dignity, not only to her wounded ego, but to humanity at large. And a woman's revenge it is, effected in meticulous machinations, climaxes and catharses and complete with the show of her one-upmanship.

Shriya is the next major character; in a way she represents the mortal manifestation of the goddess on earth. She is both the instrument of causality and agent provocateur for the plot, and thus, outweighs Lord Jagannath and Lord Balaram in terms of relative significance. She is a woman from the community of *chandaal*s. Jagannath and Balaram are the custodians of the Great Temple. Shriya is a threat to their sense of sanctity with her mere presence and hence should be kept away.

At the time of the composition of the text, the *chandaal*s stood for people from those classes who hunted and slaughtered animals, scavenge carcasses, dealt with the skin of dead animals (for making drums etc.), ate their meat and hence were untouchable. Shriya belongs to one such caste. She cleans up the palace lanes also of carcasses. Ironically, her name means beauty, and she stands for cleanliness, perseverance and discipline and order in life.

The issue of ostracization of meat-eaters is not such a charmed blemish in the historiography of the text. Because the shrine of lord Jagannath has been known for its eclecticism in religious practices. Puri temple never prohibited any Hindu because he was born to a particular community. It is also true that people who visited Puri temple did not necessarily become vegetarians.

The author's literary confusion also reflects in the characterization of lord Jagannath and lord Balaram against whom Shriya is pitted. The gods are the dwellers at the Great Temple. The author labels Them as Brahmins, the highest class in the Hindu society. Why are they Brahmins in the text? In the *Mahabharata*, Krishna is a Yadav, a cowherd and Balaram a tiller, and by successfully establishing the professed importance of farmers and other agriculturists in the political, economic and religious mainstream, the *Mahabharata* has already put these communities at pre-eminent categories of the society. Jagannath stands for Krishna; he is a cowherd and Balaram is a farmer. The author claims to be a *shudra* – one from the lowest class of Hindu society. It is almost apparent that he has depicted his characters as Brahmins so that he could show this class in an unwelcome light. Or, he has fallen back on archetypes – that a god is sacred and hence a Brahmin. Either way, taking it as his class bias or sense of awe of divinity – this is the author's projection of his conviction into his characters. Interestingly, the chief kitchen maid of Lakshmi is a Brahmin woman too, when in Puri all the servitors are from a range of castes. The author's treatment of the issue of human equality is certainly convincing, yet his treatment of the issue of class is not. While classical Sanskrit writers (most of whom were Brahmins) were capable of laughing at their Brahmin characters, Balaram Das has not transcended his class prejudice, so it looks.

Or perhaps, Balaram Das is not against any class and the text is about social interpretations. Though the righteousness of the 'Brahmin' brothers is flawed by arrogance and conceit, the socialistic content of the text stresses unity of family life, and not a summary resentment against any particular community. The text survives primarily because of its feminist concern; it is about empowering women; the arrogance of the brothers is the arrogance of the male outside any caste bias. It is in the role-reversal of lord Balaram, and not lord Jagannath, that this feminist concern attends its height and logical finish. As the elder brother, lord Balaram is the guardian of their household. Though his role is ornamental, he stands for the institution of joint-family structure of the Hindu society. Yet with his flawed wisdom he becomes the disintegrator of his own household. In the text the treatment of his plight almost borders on comicality; with quaint humor the author lampoons him, even creating a scope for subdued humor, and satire against the more serious issues of social values and institutions that should not be tampered with. By highlighting his misery more, in comparison with lord Jagannath, the author provides the comic relief and drives home the point of gender-equality more effectively.

The author's feminism is unaffected and holistic. The codes for women, which the author sets for ideal house-keeping, are extreme at times, bordering on ludicrousness and in contrast with his empathy for the class. They look anti-feminist. Goddess Lakshmi has a dark side to her too; she can be the quintessential scheming woman. She is possessive of the wedding gifts given by her father, in particular, 'the priceless four-poster', and sees no wrong in torturing her husband and brother-in-law to solace her hurt. Conversely, her action is also her fight for ascendance in the hierarchy of male power structure.

Balaram Das's repeated use of the word *chandaal* makes one to think if he is advocating for a vegetarian way of life, outside the issue of class prejudice. *Chandaal*s are primitive hunters who eat meat and hence were considered impure. They are in contrast with the gods at the temple, who are vegetarian. As though to consolidate this point, the text carries an elaborate catalogue of exquisite Odia cuisine of the exclusively vegetarian category. Indian vegetarian food includes milk and excludes every other animal product. There is not a single mention of a non-vegetarian food item in the text.

Vegetarianism in the context of Hindu society has a religious undertone to it. Gods and goddesses in Vedic literature and most of the deities of later Hinduism are vegetarian. A notable exception is goddess Kali, who is almost always described as having a terrible frightening appearance, adorned with a garland of freshly cut heads. Kali is a later addition to the Hindu pantheon (about early medieval period), and is associated with the periphery of Hindu society. According to the scriptures, she is worshipped by tribals or low-caste people – the *chandaal*s – where the worship takes place deep in the forest, and blood offerings are made to the goddess. Her temples should be built far from villages and towns, near the cremation grounds and the dwellings of *chandaal*s.

Vegetarianism as against non-vegetarianism does not sponsor hunting and slaughter. For the Hindu psyche vegetarianism opposes hunting, as Lord Krishna had been killed by Jara sabara, a hunter who mistook the lord for a deer. It is therefore not about choosing a particular class of food only. Apart from being a fact of life, it involves religiosity; when you are letting loose an arrow, you are killing a god. Lakshmi asking her devotees to stay away from non-vegetarian food on Thursdays should make particular sense beside this sub-text.

By prescribing ideal codes for women on tending family with the message to stay indoors, the author is probably directing his dissidence against the practice of mendicancy of Chaitanya Dev. The author's aversion to mendicancy and begging must have arisen from the fact that Chaitanya was herding people out of their houses to roam the streets chanting god's name deliriously and his troupe included women too. Thus the author may not be against upper classes per se as against the mendicant behavior of religious preachers of the period. And since the king Pratap Rudra Deb had also found asylum in religion, the text is also a comical, tangential shoot off against a king who was falling apart.

This is a text that advises the people of Odisha to revert back to economic activities (agriculture) instead of begging. The agricultural motifs in the worship of the goddess, the metaphor of rice, in its numerous mentions in the text, validate this point. Rice continues to be the staple agricultural crop for Odisha, where farming remains the chief source of economic activity (this applies to rural India as well). And Lakshmi is associated with crops and food, for women invoke her on a mound of new grain and recite the song written on her. I personally believe that this text had a great influence on Odisha farmers, particularly, the women, in restoring themselves to the integrity of the family, instead of roaming in the streets in the name of an unseen god under the rule of a king who had, for all practical reasons, abdicated.

Lakshmi Purana is the second major household Scriptural text in Odisha after the *Bhagavata*. Balaram Das also wrote the Odia version of Ramayana, which was not accepted as a sacred text in Odisha. The acceptance of *Lakshmi Purana* as a sacred text across Odisha, and through centuries, explains two points: one, a feminist text written by a man (and it is more difficult on the part of a man to have a feminist perspective than a woman) has appealed to a large section of women through years, though his other text, of equal sociological significance, has not been accepted. And two, the antiquity of the text, dating back to some five hundred years does not come in the way of its acceptance, belying the observation and tension in the academia that the feminist presence in literature is a recent phenomenon.

IV

Like most philosophical and religious texts all over the world, the original text of *Lakshmi Purana* is presented through dialogues. Philosophical and intellectual discourses like Vedas and Upanishads have been through dialogues. In India, where we deal with scripts and not authors, we till very recently followed this structure: a couplet with one full-stop and two full-stops. Many authors/scripts followed chapterization basing on the narrator in the text, viz., Brahma, Narada, Parashar. So for clarity for target language readers, and to avoid punctuation signs, which if used may look random and repetitive, I have done a little restructuring in translation by putting sub-chapter headings: 'Thus Spoke Parashar'. This technique is also in harmony with the format in Odia Puranas, like the *Bhagabata*.

Sub-heads have been used, too, to avoid the monotony of rendering an omniscient-narrator-narrative in the oral tradition. I have tried to avoid this monotony further by interrupting the verse format of the original, and using a blend of prose and verse in the translation, though retaining the verse format for the entire length of the text would have been easier. In the process I have formed paragraphs and dialogues out of uninterrupted oration and eased out the flexible tense patterns. The outcome has also rid the verses of their antique redundancy.

Since the text uses standard Odia, rendering it into

modern English has not caused any major problem except for a few words, in particular, the core word of the text – *chandaal*. The *chandaals* in this text refer to hunters and are not 'untouchables' in the post-British/pseudo-secular sense of the word where an untouchable is someone who carries night-soil. In fact, the Odia word for *chandaal* may have come from *hada*, bone, as the *chandaals* deal with dead animals, and hence their bones and hides. The concept of scavenging, in the present sense of the word, was not known to the Hindus at the time of composition of this text, simply as the scope for such an action never arose. It came with the Muslims; who came with their slaves, whom they made to clean toilets as their womenfolk did not go to outside for the purpose.

So I have taken certain decisions in translating. I have not translated the word as 'untouchable'. I have also decided that the tone of the rendered version of the text be made uniformly religious, keeping in view the Scriptural status the text enjoys through centuries. This has put a number of literary features of the original to test, in particular, the humor. Faint no doubt, the humor weakens in the course of translation. The repetitions in the original, effecting musicality, have been shed sometimes.

I have also used the standard addresses of the deities, viz. Lord Jagannath, Lord Balaram and Goddess Lakshmi, though the deities have been described with their numerous associations, referring to their miracles in various scriptural texts. I have been uniform in rendering the addresses of the deities, too, to avoid confusion for the target language reader, who may not be familiar with the connotation of these, associations.

The deities in the text have been addressed with reference to legends and myths of Puranas and epics.

Though goddess Lakshmi does not appear in the earliest Vedic literature, the term 'Sri' occurs quite often, and it is clear that the meanings of the term are related to the nature of the later goddess Sri-Lakshmi throughout her history. For example, in Sri-sukta, a hymn in praise of Sri in Rigveda, an important feature of Sri is her association with the lotus and the elephant, and she is described as dwelling in cow-dung and abundant in harvest. She is the goddess of beauty, royal power and good fortune. In the course of her history Sri-Lakshmi has been associated with many male deities, and by the epic period she is the consort of Vishnu and is the goddess of wealth and prosperity. According to the *Vishnu-purana*, she had been obtained from the churning of the oceans by the gods and the demons. As one born of water, she is fond of the lotus and is imaged after it. She is known as Kamalini – the lotus-faced or with her feet on a lotus flower; Padmalaya – the lotus dweller. In this text, however, she is also presented amid her other references, for example, Vaidehi, another name of Sita, the consort of Rama.

Lord Jagannath has been sometimes referred to as Krishna in the text. Jagannath, as the incarnation of Vishnu and Krishna, is dressed in yellow robes, and addressed as Govinda, Chakradhara and Hari. In the *Mahabharata*, Krishna has been fondly addressed as Kanha, Kanhai, and as Giridhari – the mountain-lifter. This has reference to the episode where Krishna as a young boy had lifted Govardhan Mountain to shelter the citizens of Gokul under it from the rains caused by a vengeful Indra, the king of heaven and the god of rains. Krishna has also been addressed as Kaliyaganjana – the vanquisher of serpent – after another of his miracles in the *Mahabharata* where as a child he had reined in a rogue underwater serpent –

Kaliya. Lord Balaram has been addressed against the same backdrop. As in the *Mahabharata*, he has been addressed in this text as Haladhara – the plough-carrier.

The temple of lord Jagannath at Puri houses three deities in its sanctum sanctorum: the brothers - Jagannath, Balabhadra - and their sister Subhadra. Goddess Lakshmi, the spouse of Jagannath resides in a separate temple, close to the main temple in the premises. The sprawling temple premise is fenced by a tall wall, known as the Meghanaada wall. This wall has four gates on all directions. The eastern gate known as the Singhadwara - the Lion Gate - is the principal entrance to the temple, and is an elaborate structure of high architectural and aesthetic standards.

The temple, known as the Great Temple, is famous for its kitchen, exclusive food items as offerings to the deities and dining hall. The deities are offered cooked food for lunch, which are then sold as 'Prasad' inside the temple premises. The dining space of the temple, a section of which serves as the space for sale of 'prasad', is large, with capacity to accommodate thousands of pilgrims.

The temple at Puri mixes everyday reality and matters of divinity with an amazing ambivalence. Incredible anecdotes on the mystery of the deities and stories involving real people and places cohabit to add to the temple lore with rolling of years. The deities are gods, yet they are quite human too. Balaram Das has built his text on these local legends and practices of the temple. As characters, he presents the deities in the tradition of the temple practices. Goddess Lakshmi, the protagonist, can grant 'a million auspicious cows' as boons to her devotees. She too is entitled to alimony of 'rice grains and other essentials' at the imminent separation from her husband. As the deities are representative of the Odia consciousness, rituals of standard Odia festivities are observed in the temple and the deities participate in them. Conversely, the rites and festivities practiced by the deities must have shaped the list of festivals and rituals of Odisha. Thus lord Jagannath and lord Balaram fast on *Ekadashi* – the eleventh day of each lunar fortnight, and therefore, relish an elaborate special dinner on the previous day. In fact, it is one such day the crisis in the plot of the text begins with, when lord Jagannath is asking goddess Lakshmi to return early as she has to cook the meal of the day because the following day will be Ekadashi – one of fasting for the bothers.

Gundicha temple is the abode of the mother of Jagannath. The journey to this temple is taken up every year by the deities of the Great Temple during Rath Yatra. Lakshmi does not accompany the deities on this journey, as Jagannath does not inform her about his trip. A wife does not like the husband to go to his ancestral place. This metaphor of rejection of the visit of the God to his maternal place by his wife is yet another example of the text, which probably sends a message to the wives: do not prevent the husband from taking care of his mother.

I have always felt the need to justify my transliteration of Odia words. Let me site an example. In case of Odia language the phoneme in the second syllable of 'Parva' (festival) is /b/. Thus 'Parva' is 'Parba' in Odia, and both /v/ and /b/ are bilabial in Odia phonetics. In Sanskrit, this phoneme is /w/ which is a labio-dental sound, though in Sanskrit too both /b/ and /v/ are bi-labial. So unless the case is that of proper nouns, I prefer to transliterate Odia words with /b/ in place of /v/ or /w/; for example, 'Adi Parba' and not 'Adi Parva' as is the popular practice. This is for discernment, clarity and beauty of a language as against the syndrome of aligning with an accepted practice for convenience and summary evaluation. The variations in spellings of words across the text should be understood in this light.

I have transliterated 'Dasa' as Das, the way the word is spoken when used as a surname. (Accordingly, 'Deba' has been 'Deb') Perhaps the palm-leaf calligraphy of the period did not find it convenient to write the word as 'Das' as the inscription would have required an added sign indicating the inflexion.

Lipipuspa Nayak

LAKSHMI PURANA
A Paean to the Goddess of Fortune

Praise to you, O Lakshmi,
the cherished daughter of seven oceans.
I fold my hands before you a thousand times,
Lakshmi, the consort of Lord Vishnu
and the Goddess of His house.
Praise to you, Kamala, the epitome of kindness,
as day after day you rear matters and beings
which move and do not move, and the lowliest insects.
With your infinitesimal grace,
a poor person comes to infinite riches,
and outshines Kubera, the rich man of the three worlds.
Those who court animus towards you, Mother,
they strive in vain for a morsel of rice;
how much so ever they earn, they remain hungry.
If someone listens to this episode with attention,
or sings it aloud with divine devotion,
he is cured of his penury;
as you, the goddess of great miracles, are always
pleased with him.

Therefore Mother!
at your feet my countless genuflections;
please fulfill my wishes, I plead before you.
Let me knit together,
this laconic hymn of your holy grace;
bestow upon me some divine afflatus
so that I may compose this paean,
O the mother of the universe.

The Paean

One day the two sages Narada and Parashar set out on one of their regular tours of the universe. After wandering around, in due course, they arrived in a village. It was a Thursday in the month of Margashira, the eighth lunar month of the Hindu calendar, and all the villagers were celebrating this festive day. Every household had been cleaned and consecrated with the paste of cow-dung and water. The floors and walls had been painted with the paste of rice powder and water, with designs of lotus and footprints of Goddess Lakshmi. The women of the households had bathed thoroughly and were attired in saris of fine cotton and fine silk. They were completely immersed in the worship of Lakshmi. They had breached the caste hierarchy too; from the Brahmins to the lower castes – everyone was engrossed in the invocation of the goddess. The ululation of women welcoming Goddess Lakshmi filled up the sky.

Narada was one of the sons of Brahma, the lord of Creation. Narada witnessed the rituals and the festivities, and enquired from Parashar with impatience: "Tell me, O great ascetic, what is this event? People of all castes have come together to celebrate this joyous festival! Are they observing some vow? Are they undertaking a penance? Which god or goddess are they worshipping? What are the canons prescribed for this ritual?"

Thus Spoke Parashar

Parashar smiled softly, and said: "Be calm my dear Pupil of rituals, and let me answer your questions. They have devoted the Thursday of Margashira for worship of Lakshmi, the Goddess of wealth and prosperity. This Thursday is also known as Paddy Thursday because after harvesting and threshing, paddy comes inside the houses of farmers from the field on this day. The people here are in a mood of abnegation to propitiate Lakshmi. Margashira is the essence of all the twelve months. The Thursdays of this month are dear to Lakshmi, the first Thursday being the dearest. If a Thursday of this month coincides with the tenth lunar day of the waxing phase, it is the occasion for *Sudasha Vrata,* the day you must devote to worship for prosperity and wellbeing. Goddess Lakshmi is particularly fond of this day."

After narrating this Parashar went into a spell of silence.

Narada asked: "Who has observed this penance for Goddess Lakshmi? And what benediction was bestowed upon him? And do you know anyone who professed animosity with the Goddess and earned her wrath? Please tell me, O the king of austerities; I am pining for these revelations."

Parashar listened to Narada and became happy. He was blissful and his speech was mellifluous. "You're great, Narada," he said. "You are blessed and sacred as you have evinced interest in the Goddess and the rituals of Her supplication. Let me narrate some ancient anecdotes. You will be ecstatic to hear these anecdotes.

"One day Lakshmi was with Lord Jagannath, her husband. With folded hands, she informed him: 'Lord, today is the day of my veneration on the earth. If you so permit, I'll visit the city.'

'Lakshmi, you must tour the city only,' said Lord Jagannath. You'll have to return in time and prepare the meal of the tenth lunar day, as tomorrow is the *Ekadasi*, the eleventh lunar day and I have to fast.'

Lakshmi listened to every word of the Lord. With great care she attired herself for the divine sojourn and put on ornaments:

> She fixed to her nose lobes nose-rings of nine jewels;
> Her neckline embellished with
> the four-stringed gemstone necklace;
> Elegant armlets and bracelets bedecked
> her arms and wrists;
> Pendants of cat's eye dangled from threads of gold;
> Anklets of jingling bells adorned her ankles;
> The Mother looked gorgeous with these jewels
> and a lot more other ornaments.
> Since the Mother owns the three worlds
> of earth, heaven
> and hell,
> How can we describe her jewels and ornaments?

"Therefore, dear Narada, let me have your undivided attention, as I narrate the tale of Mother Lakshmi before you.

"The Mother, who is also the mother of Creation slipped into the guise of an old Brahmin woman and materialized at the house of a seafarer. His wife had stood at the porch of the house. Maha Lakshmi, the great Goddess told her: 'Listen to me, O prosperous woman, and compose yourself. Today is the first Thursday of Margashira, the day of supplicating Goddess Lakshmi. Why have you kept your house unkempt?'

The wife of the seafarer asked immediately: 'How does one observe the day, and for whom? Please, Brahmin Sister, do elaborate. If I'm convinced, I'll observe the vow"'

Thus Spoke Lakshmi

Then Padmalaya, another name for Goddess Lakshmi because her abode is *Padma*, the blooming lotus, said with utmost serenity: Listen to me O prosperous woman, as I prescribe the practices and rituals for the worship of Goddess Lakshmi.

On the first Thursday of Margashira, you must hasten to leave your bed long before the sun rises, and plaster the floors of your house and the yards with cow-dung and water. Then you draw the footmarks of goddess Lakshmi amidst lotus petals with paste of rice powder and water. Fetch a new bamboo bowl that you use for measuring paddy, clean it and make it dry so that you can draw on it murals with rice powder. Grind some rice to make a paste for the purpose of drawing these motifs. Then you must bathe from head to toe and cleanse the impurities of body and mind.

Now you get a wooden chair or a small pedestal. Wash it clean. Build a small heap of freshly harvested paddy on the pedestal. Remember, the fresh paddy should not be of the black variety; it should be white. Place some of this paddy in a brass measuring pot to the brim. Place three betel nuts, rinsed in turmeric and water, on the measuring pot. Take some paddy stalks, weave the stalks into a plait and hang it over the pot. Then adorn the pedestal with colorful silk draperies, flowers, betel nuts, sugarcane, radish and plantains.

Then Lady, invoke Maha Lakshmi, the Great Goddess. You must offer fragrant flowers, camphor, aromatic incense and earthen lamps. First you must offer this early morning prayer, then the offerings to the young goddess, and finally the offering to the goddess who was already satiated - in the same way as three meals of offerings follow one another before Lord Jagannath.

The Goddess too has another benedictory day for her devotees, so that they can keep penance and propitiate her. This day is renowned in the three worlds as *Sudasha Vrata*, the day of security and happiness of mankind. If the tenth lunar day of the waxing phase of the moon falls on a Thursday, it is the day of *Sudasha Vrata*. On this day too, you have to wake up before daybreak and wash the floors and walls of your house like I have said earlier, and draw murals and prints of lotus patterns on them. Then after taking bath, outline a circular lotus theme and place there a small throne. Then fetch the betel nut, used in the oblation rituals of the Goddess, and wash the nut with the holy concoction of curd, milk, honey, ghee and jaggery. Get ten hanks of thread and loop ten knots along its length chanting the name of the Goddess each time. Roll the thread around ten stalks of sacred creeper grass, and place it beside the consecrated betel nut. If you have been observing this penance already, then you can use the same thread, dear sister. This thread is known as *Vrata* or Penance. Now remember carefully that you must offer the following:

Soak one measure of raw rice in water. After a few hours, grind the rice carefully to a powder, and cook the powdered rice in boiling water. Knead the mixture into a smooth dough. Prepare the stuffing made of at least ten ingredients: like cheese, banana, coconut, molasses and spices. Put this stuffing inside balls of the rice powder dough, make the stuffed balls spherical and steam them over boiling water. Then with a heart filled with devotion, offer the spherical cakes to the Goddess, and eat only these cakes - her benediction - and be at peace. You must not share the cakes with others. Even your own daughter who is married off, shall not be proffered the offering you have made to your Goddess.

And now, you wife of a seafarer, let me have your attention! I'll now brief you about the taboos you must shun on a Thursday:

Never roast rice on a Thursday to make pop rice.
If a woman on a Thursday
gluttonizes on food that is not vegetarian,
or does not wash her hair,
or eats food left over by someone,
or applies oil to her hair;
Maha Lakshmi, the Great Goddess
will certainly knock down her pranks.

If on a Thursday
a woman spins thread from cotton,
or eats a dish of gourd and fish, or
sleeps in the shadow of a cot,
or savors after sunset
a meal of curd and rice,
she never has the blessings of Maha Lakshmi.

On such a Thursday anyone who
goes to the barber's for a shave or a haircut,

or throws away food that he cannot eat,
does not win the blessings of Lakshmi, the Goddess.
If on the morning of a Thursday,
a woman does not daub with cow-dung
the floor of her gateway
because she is indolent,
or does not scoop out ash from her hearth,
and eats non-vegetarian food,
she earns the Goddess's wrath.
 Lakshmi takes away her wealth
and people,
and even as she goes begging
no one gives her either food or cloth.
A woman attired in white
on a Thursday comes to enjoy
enormous wealth and luck smiles on her.
On Thursdays
if a woman spanks her child,
or washes her cooking pots in such a manner
that they still bear the smoke stain;
or lights the evening wicks before the tulsi plant
long after the dusk,
she suffers loss of wealth and children
and eternal deprivation.
On Thursdays
a woman who eats food roasted on fire,
or spreads out a crooked bed,
or disobeys her in-laws, or sleeps naked,
they are all cursed.
If a man ploughs his field on a new moon day
or on the first day of a solar month
of the Hindu calendar,
or on these days puts oil to his hair,

he too is cursed.
If a man tells a lie in the village court,
or gets down to dinner without washing his feet,
if a woman shears a pumpkin,
if a man makes love to a menstruating woman –
they too are cursed.
When a man does not invoke
the souls of his ancestors
in the months of Virgo and Libra,
or breaks into giggles whenever he speaks:
such men invariably suffer unhappiness.
Their lives become shorter
And they starve.
There are three days of a month –
Thursday, the new moon day and the first day
of the solar month –
if a husband and wife eat together
on any of these nights,
or if a woman indulges in desire for man
on any of these days and nights,
shunning restraint and religious propriety,
they do not die alright,
but are led through endless streets
of sorrow and deprivation;
they wander everywhere for food and rag in vain.
People must not eat bitter gourd or neem
on these three days.
If they do, they shall be persecuted
at the door of Yama –
the god of death and *dharma* –
when they die.
If a woman keeps penance on these days,
and donates generously to the distressed

and the deprived,
and fasts on these Thursdays,
she adds to her riches, family,
fame and years.
The one who does not wash his face
after waking up in the morning,
must not show his face to others
as it does not usher well for others.
The one who, after getting up,
goes back to the stale bed,
is forsaken squarely by Lakshmi.
One who sits on the floor to eat
and does not use a mat,
one overcome with sexual drive
in the presence of a virgin,
one who faces either west or south as he eats -
Lakshmi deserts these men.
Lakshmi never takes kindly to
a woman who coifs her hair in the twilight hours.
Those who do not rinse
their mouths after taking food,
those who dine in dark rooms,
those who massage oil after taking bath,
those who scratch the earth with finger nails,
those who fan themselves with ends of their sarees -
Lakshmi never bestows a glance
at the countenance of such women.
A woman who is always angry with her husband,
a woman who never ever obeys her husband,
an adulteress,
a woman who remains filthy and unwashed –
Lakshmi does not bestow a glance
on their faces.

Such women become paupers
begging for food from house to house.
The house where a cantankerous,
lazy, tomboyish and acerbic woman lives,
who has no respect for a Brahmin,
guest and god –
such a house is indeed, a cremation ground,
and Lakshmi always forsakes such a place.
A woman who does not take care of her husband
with devotion,
will endure in her future rebirths
the pain that her husband suffers.
If a woman takes care of her husband
like he is her god;
careful of what he likes and dislikes,
thoroughly cleanses her body,
 and is equal and fair to the elders and the young
in the family,
and is impartial when she serves food for
each member in the family,
and never lets a word of her husband fall on the floor;
and suffers every sorrow that her husband endures
and revels in his happiness –
Lakshmi never leaves
the home of such a woman.
Lakshmi shall not ever see with her own eyes
such a pious woman's unhappiness.
Such a pious woman enjoys endless happiness
in this earth
adorned with husband, son, daughter and wealth;
at the end of this earthly sojourn,
such a pious woman spends every moment
with the Goddess

in Baikuntha, the abode of Vishnu in heaven,
immersed in eternal pleasure and bliss.
A married woman whose husband is alive
has no other destination in life,
but the husband;
meditation, religious rituals, and repeating god's name
may not be for her the right principles of life.
A woman who resorts to senseless penances
and neglects her family and husband,
becomes a child-widow in every rebirth
after this life.
A woman
who looks after the guests of the family
without rancor or equivocation,
is termed as a woman of virtues by the Scriptures.
Sri Lakshmi is always and ever attached
to these women and men,
who do not abdicate the *dharma*
of their ancestors and remain righteous.
Women have no deliverance
without serving their husbands.
A woman who devotes herself to her husband,
reaches after her death
the land of the gods.
Even the worship of Lakshmi
and other penances and pilgrimages,
with neglect of the husband and family,
are ironies and will not salvage such women.
If a vainglorious woman evades duty to her husband,
and refrains on Thursdays
from worshipping Lakshmi,
she risks her wellbeing in this life
and through all her future rebirths;

she wanders through lives of unhappiness, grief and ailments.

Thus the Goddess spoke to the wife of the seafarer and ordained: 'Go and perform the Penance for appeasement of Lakshmi right away, or else you will be deprived of all your wealth. And you will be in misery without food and clothes.'

Thus Spoke Parashar

"Now, listen carefully, Narada," continued Parashar, "the Goddess finished her discourse before the wealthy woman and moved on. She covered a long path, stopping at each home and every household, but nowhere did she find the sacrosanct environ she was looking for. In one house, a young maiden lay on a bed in a deep slumber. Another maiden was so overwhelmed by sleep that her robes had fallen off exposing her body. Elsewhere a woman's tresses had splayed on the floor while she was asleep. Thus Maha Lakshmi took account of the spectacle and left for the lane where the *chandaal*s – the poor who performed menial duties – lived.

Shriya, a woman in that lane of *chandaals,* lived outside Puri, the premises of the kingdom of Lord Jagannath. And lo! Her greatness as a devotee was not known to the gods. She swept clean the streets of the kingdom of Lord Jagannath everyday with rapturous devotion for the Lord.

On that day, Shriya had left her bed when the night was still in its third quarter and fetched the dung of a single-colored cow from the streets. With the dung and water she had swabbed the floor of her house and veranda in meticulous swathes. She had also sprinkled a few drops of the urine she had collected from a calf, and had consecrated her house further. Then she drew murals on the floor of her house with raw rice paste. She drew an intricate lotus motif with sixteen petals. She lighted a wicker lamp filled with ghee that had ten mouths to bear ten wicks, placing it at the center of the mural. On this mural, she spread out fruits and tubers of ten colors. She kept a thread of ten hanks on this. She became restive and fetched raw rice and ten stems of *duba*, the creeper grass. She also offered incense, burning wicks dipped in ghee, sacred food, flowers, and aromatic oil on the patterns she had drawn. Then, she invoked the gods:

> I worship you O Lakshmi and Jagannath!
> Glory be to You, Mother, the homemaker of Hari,
> Hari is the Emperor of the Universe.
> I am ignorant in the matters of religious rituals
> as I am from a low servile caste, and on top of that,
> I live in the Lane of the Chandaals,
> and l am a Chandaal woman.
> O Lotus-faced Mother please deign
> to accept my veneration.

Lakshmi, Vishnu's Maharani was passing by along the main street. She could not ignore the pleadings of the *chandaal* woman and was moved with her piety. The lotus motif in the house too tempted Lakshmi. So she entered the house of the *chandaal* woman, and materialized on the lotus motif. The entire household of the poor woman glittered to an unusual radiance in the presence of Lakshmi, and when the Goddess had graced the house, how can I even think of a metaphor to narrate the splendor of the spectacle?

'Now, dear Shriya,' said Lakshmi, 'ask and carry for yourself a boon, since I've been pleased with you. I promise you, I'll wipe out your woes.'

The poor woman tells, her hand placed on her head:

'What can I ask for?
I do not know how to ask for a boon.
Well, give me a billion auspicious cows.
Give me riches Mother,
which should measure up only to Kuber's,
provide son to my lap,
give enough gold bangles and armlets
to cover both my hands,
and make me immortal through the four eons
of Satya, Dwapara, Treta and Kali, the eon of sin.'

Lakshmi heard her and said: 'You have lost your head. I can give you all you have asked for except that I have no power to bestow on you immortality. How could you ask for this boon? You will wallow in immeasurable wealth as long as you live. After your life on this earth expires, you will reach at the abode of Vishnu. Keep this Penance for me every day; let your being lie at the feet of Lakshmi-Narayan.'

Parashar continued the narration before sage Narada:

Out there Lord Jagannath and Lord Balaram had been to the woods for a hunt. The episode of Lakshmi and the poor woman Shriya was revealed to Balaram when he sat in meditation."

The Conversation Between Balaram and Jagannath

Lord Balaram called out his younger brother Lord Jagannath and said: 'Look at the ways of your wife, Hari, she has visited the house of a *chandaal* woman. She goes around the houses of people from lower castes who skin dead animals, who scavenge and who make drums with the skins of dead animals. Thereafter she enters our Grand Temple without taking bath.

'And she does this every day, and makes us, the brothers, outcasts of society. Since she carries the title *the-redeemer-of-the-poor*, she cannot bear the poor to suffer. She has graced the house of the woman *chandaal* as the low-caste woman has been worshipping at her feet on the day of *Sudasha Vrata*, the propitiatory penance in her honour. My dear Krishna, if you so need your wife, hurry up and erect a palace in the lane of the *chandaals*. Or else, listen to our words and chase her away. If you pamper a spouse like Lakshmi, we will run into destitution and eternal deprivation.'

Hari listened to his brother's palaver and said: 'You suggest that we chase her out of the Grand Temple. But how and where will we ever get another homemaker like her after that? If she has erred, let me offer a suggestion for her atonement: let us invite respectfully the gods from the heaven. Let's spend five hundred thousand rupees to hold the ritual of absolution and re-induct Lakshmi to our society. And yet, if we find her flouting the principles and rituals of the Temple again, we will drive her out from there – this is my pledge before you, Elder Brother; after all the Princess of the Ocean has made a mistake without her knowledge – wouldn't you forgive her for once, Brother?'

Balaram said: 'Listen to me Govinda, you are also called Bhavagrahi, the one who understands emotions. If your Lakshmi stays in the Temple, I will not. Wife is like the shoe adorning the foot of a husband. If I have a brother, I can always find a billion wives for him. If you are obsessed with your wife, O Krishna, construct a royal mansion in the *Chandaals*' Lane. Don't come to my Grand Temple again, keep off its borders along with your woman.'

Jagannath, the lord of the universe, could no longer stand the upbraiding of his elder brother. 'I shall leave her,' he said, and his lips became scarlet. He retired to the Temple, paused at the entrance, the Lion Gate, and breathed out deeply looking upwards.

Thus Spoke Parashar

Hark, Narada! There Shriya had been worshipping at the painting of the feet of Lakshmi. The Goddess was pleased with the devotion of Shriya and bestowed boons on her. Shriya used to live in a hut which resembled a wasp's burrow and with the blessings of Lakshmi, it turned into a palace of sandalwood. Her house, which never had food grains for the next meal, was now stacked with pure gold at every corner. The woman, in whose house a son never played, now bore five sons with the blessings of the Goddess. 'Possess more prosperity and many more sons,' the Goddess blessed Shriya and proceeded on her divine sojourn.

The *chandaal* woman came to luck because of Lakshmi. Now Narada, you must track attentively the strings of this remarkable tale.

The Conversation between Lakshmi and Jagannath

Lakshmi, the spinner of great miracles, appeared at the Lion Gate of the Temple. She saw the two brothers Lord Jagannath and Lord Balaram covering the entrance. 'Let me get in,' she said, 'as I have to cook the special meal of the day, and today is the holy tenth day of the lunar month.'

'Have you lost your head?' asked Jagannath, her

husband. 'Why did you visit the street of the *chandaals*? I did not see this, but Elder Brother has seen you there. Had it been I, I would have covered up your misdeed. Lakshmi! You may go away now; we have no further business with you. Brother has upbraided me enough because of what you have done.

'He says: *Lakshmi is with the chandaals. Lakshmi goes to the house of the sinners. She does not take bath after her trips to these habitations, and enters the Temple, polluted. There is no sinner worse than her in the world.*

'Therefore, Soul-mate! Listen to my words. Everyone in the three worlds calls you the queer goddess. In spite of being the goddess of my household, you roam like a queer woman. You unite a thousand homes to make one; you break one home to a thousand ones. Such are your divine dispensations and miracles. Now go away, Lakshmi, don't live in my Abode. Elder Brother is infuriated with you.'

Goddess Lakshmi looks the Lord of the Universe in the eye and speaks: 'Give me a divorce first and then throw me out of the Temple.'

Jagannath, the Lord of the Universe looks at Lakshmi, and says: 'We do not follow the practice of divorce in our social rank and caste. We do not look at the wife in the face when we ask her to leave.'

Goddess Lakshmi gazes at the face of the Lord and speaks: 'Lord! Just recall the days when you went and churned the oceans. You acquired me from the waters among the chanting of the Vedas and the hymns. You have forgotten everything that happened then. My father Varuna, the god of the Oceans, consecrated you and married you to me on an altar made of gold. He gave his daughter to you and accepted your suzerainty over the Demons. He also beseeched that you must forgive the first ten mistakes of his daughter, the ten mistakes that I, as a woman, am likely to commit during life. And forget ten, you did not forgive me even for one mistake and for this lapse, you reproached me calling me a *chandaaluni*, a lowly woman!

'And do you remember the day following our wedding, when we settled down for the Game of Cowrie? We were playing with cowries, garden shells made of gold. I placed the cowries on the floor seven times, and every time you placed the shells on my palms. I clasped the shells in my closed fist, which, as per the rules of the game, you were to open. But you, the Lord of the Universe, could not unlock my fist, and in turn said: *Ask me for any favor you want from me, Goddess! Whatever you wish for, shall of course be proffered by me, Soul-mate.* And I had replied with folded palms: *Let me have your undivided attention, Lord of the Universe, as I ask for a favor from you. The eighth day since our wedding will be a Thursday, and this is my day. On this day, I'll grace and serve food at all the homes on earth, and serve food to everyone from the lowliest insects to the Supreme Brahman. And you shall not, Lord, grudge in your heart this act of mine.* On that day, from your divine mouth you vowed: *So be it.* And, Lord, how can you recant now?'

Lord Jagannath flared up with anger and said: 'Your father is an accumulation of salt and he is wasting himself away with the incessant roaring of the waves. And you, his daughter, are squint-eyed and your failings are too many to be narrated. Who can stand the way your father bellows all the time? That's why we two brothers have erected the high and tough Meghanaad Wall around our fortress and have retreated to the quietude of the Temple.'

Lakshmi peered into the face of Lord Jagannath and said: 'Yes, I'd appeared for a while at an outcaste's home. And you want to refuse me entry to the Temple because an outcaste is socially ostracized. You also ridiculed me because of my class, pedigree and *gotra*. Now Lord, let me also attempt to reply – I know that I cannot exhaust the full details about your caste and past: it is true that because you lord over the universe, the truth about your clan and ancestry are not revealed. In real, you have no definite identity of your caste or roots. For one, both you brothers were born and reared in the families of cowherds. You have taken rice in the house of Nima, the mercenary, who was from the dubious caste of the most loathsome of slaves. You had gone to the city of Hastina as an Emissary of the Pandavas, and only people from low castes become emissaries because they are not to be killed. There you had your meal at the place of Bidura who has a tainted parentage. And what about Jara Sabar, the tribesman who worshipped you in his jungle abode for ten years? He fetched fruits and tubers from the jungle, bit into them to taste, kept aside the fruits that tasted bitter and alkaloid and offered the sweet ones to you. So you were hungry and eager for the leftovers of a *sabar* and lost your caste. Both of you. What selective amnesia you have! You brothers are the sinners; yet you spread canards about others. And you do not weigh virtue alongside vice. If a wife commits a mistake, the husband stands by her; does a master sack his servant because the servant made a mistake for the first time? Why don't you ordain justice like this, Lord? Instead, you are repeatedly asking me to go away!'

Lord Jagannath speaks: 'Let me do something like this. We shall provide you food and other essentials on a daily basis. Later we will persuade elder brother to show favour. Then we will bring you back. We can never defy our Brother.'

Goddess Lakshmi speaks: 'I don't beg for your alms.

I am going away almost an orphan; a wife who could not be given protection by her husband. I am not the daughter of a widow or a woman with ill omen. I'll be setting out for my father's house. Before I do that, Lord, take back the ornaments you had given me, so that you don't blame me later.'

The Lord says: 'Are you mad Lakshmi? Why should we take away your ornaments? Does a husband ever denude his wife of the jewelry given to her?'

The Goddess looks at the sacred face of her husband and speaks:

'I am your first married wife, always remember this. Don't allege, *Lakshmi lived in my house; She made away with ornaments worth thousands of golden rupees.* Don't let loose on me, Lord, such infamy; take back the ornaments you once presented me.'

Parashar Speaks

Lakshmi untied the pearl tassel from her hair;
She took off the royal veil of fine silk
embroidered with gold and gemstones.
The Mother unfastened her netted waistband
of gemstones and jewels;
She took out the pearl nose rings.
From both her ears, she took off
the large diamond danglers;
she took out her jade and gold necklace.
The goddess took out her anklets
of fine filigreed silver;
she hastened to dislodge the rings off her toes.
Now how to describe her other jewelry sets?
When piled together
the gem stones and jewels and the ornaments radiated.

Lakshmi heaped the ornaments at one corner;
'Keep these,' she said, 'O Friend of the Poor.'

Lord Jagannath replies: 'What shall we do with these? We have no need for the ornaments. When a householder has to sadly separate from his wife, he has to provide for her food and clothing for six months. Carry along these jewelry, so that you can sell or exchange the ornaments off to feed and clothe yourself.'

Goddess Lakshmi speaks:
'Listen to me, carefully,
O you God of the Universe!
When you bring home another wife like me,
present her these ornaments.
I am leaving fallen and unsheltered;
but bear my curse, Jagannath, the omniscient -
if the sun and the moon really move in the universe,
let you, Jagannath, the master of the universe,
be denied a morsel of rice.
For twelve years pitiable you shall remain,
dispossessed of food, clothing and water;
You, the vanquisher of Kaliya,
the underwater serpent,
will get something to eat
only when it is served by me,
a defiled *chandaal* woman.'

The Revenge of Lakshmi

Thus the Goddess spewed a curse and walked out. She walked out of the Temple and walked along alone. The maids who waited on her in the palace followed her. The Goddess addressed them: *I am going away since I have been condemned to dishonor and abandoned by Lakshmi; but why are you following me?*

Then she reflected: If I go to my father's house now, I can't stay there for more than four days. Because Lord Jagannath shall come there to meet his father-in-law, and when my father sees Lord Jagannath, he will surely hand me over to the Lord. My curse will go in vain and the Greatest of the Gods will not experience destitution.

Thus then goddess mulled over her options. She remembered Vishwakarma, the architect of the universe. At that moment Vishwakarma happened to be in Baikuntha, the abode of Vishnu in Heaven. Vishwakarma made himself available at her command instantly and prayed: 'Do assign me a duty, O the goddess of great miracles!'

The goddess looked at Vishwakarma and proclaimed: 'The Lord has called me a lowly woman and has thrown me out of the palace. Will you build a humble adobe hut for me?'

Vishwakarma rushed as soon as he received orders from the goddess and erected a mansion of length and breadth each six miles. He built the walls of each room of the mansion with gold and studded every wall with diamonds, jades and rubies. Pearls glistened from the joints of the beams and rafters, which were supported by pillars of corals. Lakshmi, the lotus-faced expressed her immense satisfaction and praise to Vishwakarma for his work and the architect then headed back for Baikuntha, in heaven.

Then the goddess sent for the Octad of Spooks and ordained: 'My dear Octad of Spooks, do as I ask you to. First you enter the kitchen of the palace at the Grand Temple, and devour the sixty platters of offerings ready for the deities. Then consume the thirteen dishes of curry including spinach with green gram; the sweet and bitter buttermilk cooked with mustard paste. You must partake the sour cooked thick curd with plenty of sugar candy.

Then you must taste the delectable items of the divine banquet that has the taste of nectar. After you have finished all the food, you gather the earthen cooking pots and hurl them over each other. Thereafter enter the treasure house of the palace and fetch the wealth of five hundred and twenty million cartloads. Make sure that you don't leave out even the tiniest unit of currency, and hand over the possessions to me.'

The Spooks looked at the face of the Great Goddess and said: 'How can we do that? Lord Jagannath is bound to be awake and he will overpower and curse us.'

So Lakshmi, the lotus-faced, summoned Nidravati - the Goddess of sleep - and said: 'Listen to my request, my sister! Go and overwhelm the brothers with sleep till forenoon tomorrow.'

The Goddess of sleep left to carry out the commands. She engulfed Lord Jagannath and Balaram with sleep. The spooks entered the kitchen of the palace and gorged on the food there. After engorging themselves, they gathered the earthen pots and hurled them to the ground. Then the octad entered the storehouse of the palace and emptied the room of its fifty-two billion items of wealth. The haulage continued late into the night, and after about sixteen hours the spooks had carted away each asset of the palace, down to a winnow and a sweeping broom, to the palace of Lakshmi.

The goddess was pleased with the spooks. 'Today you have done the duty of a son,' she said and commended on their feat. 'But where is my treasure four-poster?' she asked them. 'The four- poster costs five hundred thousand gold coins. Go dear Spirits, fetch the bed for me. If Lord Jagannath does not ask for me anymore, the men in this world too will not need women. If the Lord does not build his nest with me again, men too will outgrow their need for women in the Kaliyug.'

'The two brothers are lying on the four-poster,' the spooks submitted. 'Balaram carries the prowess of a billion lions; then there is the Lord of the universe who has crushed Kaliya, the serpent of the oceans. There are seven great mountains, and of them one is the immovable great mountain, Lord Jagannath.'

'Then do like as I say,' said Maha Lakshmi, the Great Goddess. 'Bring a cot of twined hemp-ropes. Roll the two brothers on to the cot and then ferry out the gem four-poster.'

So the spooks dashed off to the palace again. They placed a hemp cot near the four-poster and lifted Lord Balaram first. They rolled his slumbering form on to it. Then they did the same with Lord Jagannath. After transferring the brothers to the hemp cot, they fetched and ferried the gem four-poster to Lakshmi's abode. They also fetched for the Goddess the robes of fine silk that the brothers had worn. The Goddess was contended now. 'Now dear Spirits,' she bestowed her benediction on them, 'I'm pleased with your service to no end. Hence, even if you have not asked for anything for yourselves, let me grant you a boon - go to Baikuntha and dwell there happily.'

The blessed spirits left for the celestial abode forthwith.

The Goddess hatched another plan. She invoked Saraswati, the Goddess of learning, and the other wife of Vishnu. She asked Saraswati: 'Dear Saraswati, please do something for me. Make an elaborate tour of the worlds so that you visit every house in each province. I can foresee that Lord Jagannath will visit every household begging for food. And there, you grace the vocal chords of every person so that they refuse Him rice and water. The Lord will remember me only when He has suffered such ordeal.'

Parashar Speaks

There Lord Jagannath and Lord Balaram had a very comfortable sleep and woke up from the deep slumber four hours after daybreak. 'Aye Jagannath,' said Balaram, 'I don't hear a noise around, not even the voice of Mudi Ratha, our chief servitor and custodian of the sanctum sanctorum. Where have the chambermaids gone? Where are the Temple clerks and the servants? There is no water even to wash our face. What do we do, tell me Jagannath.'

Lord Jagannath replied: 'Great Brother! Such things happen when one is deserted by Goddess Lakshmi.'

'Listen younger brother! Must you talk like that about your silly wife?' asserted Balaram. When someone's wife sulks and makes herself scarce, doesn't her house-master himself cook food?'

Then the brothers went into the storeroom. The room was absolutely empty. 'What has happened?' yelled Balaram. 'What happened to the fifty-two billion treasures of the palace? Even when millions of people are provided food from this store, the stock never runs out. And who could have emptied the store house in such a short span of time?'

As they rummaged through the room, Balaram found a gold ring and secured it in the end of his cloth, carefully tying the end with seven knots. 'Did you get something, Great Brother?' asked Jagannath.

Balaram said: 'I have got riches, that is a gold ring.'

Jagannath said: 'Brother, why are you preserving a worthless lump of brass?'

Balaram replied: 'What turn of events! The gold ring that I had found turned to low quality brass! The ornament that had been carved out of pure gold, did not measure up to a damaged cowrie, that is our twisted fate!'

The brothers walked out of the storeroom and went to the Divine Kitchen. Balaram stood at the door and Jagannath went inside. Black soot of the kitchen smeared his face and body. The face of the Lord, that had always been dark, shone more with the coating of soot.

'Listen to me Jagannath,' Balaram said. 'The world calls you the glutton belly-god. So now you are gorging all the rice there, all by yourself, without sparing for me a grain.'

The younger God sulked: 'Listen Great Brother! Where do I get rice, when there is no sight of even the hearth? Why must you talk like this before you understand the reality?'

Then the Brothers went and inspected the Divine Granary. The granary that stored millions of tons of rice did not have even an empty husk. The Brothers, desolate and downcast, arrived at the banks of Indradyumna, the Temple Pond, and alas! There was not a drop of water in the Pond. So the Brothers returned to the Grand Temple. The Gods accepted this as a ritual fast and went to sleep.

The next day when the Brothers woke up from sleep long after the daybreak, they could find no water to wash their faces.

'My wits have failed - what do we do now?' asked Balaram. 'We have spent the whole of yesterday without food. Today there is no strength in our body to walk one step. If we don't manage to get some cooked rice from somewhere today, we will not be able to remain alive.

'Let me have your attention, dear,' Balaram continued.

'Let's go and beg inside our kingdom so that we can save our lives.'

So the Brothers draped themselves with upper apparels reduced to rags, and sacred threads. They carried tumbledown parasols and set out. They did not get water to prepare a paste of sandalwood, to draw *tilak* on their foreheads, which would identify them as Brahmin mendicants. Wherever they went asking for water, they were taken for purloiners and prowlers and were threatened with assault and chased away. And thus the terrified Brothers fled the streets immediately.

'Let's go to the house of the Chief Servitor, Elder Brother!' suggested Jagannath.

So the Brothers, hand in hand, walked towards their Chief Servitor's house and reached his house. Two Brahmins have rushed to our quarters,' said the daughter-in-law of the house to her mother-in-law. The mother-in-law, a widow, could not recognize the brothers. She closed the doors on their face, and howled: 'Gather round, with staffs and sticks; let's hound away these two bandits, or burglars, O women folk, or whatever.'

The terrified Brothers left the gates of the house and chanted hymns from the Sama and Yajur Vedas from a distance. With their hymns, the dried and dead shrubs and trees blossomed. The Brahmin widow realized that they were Brahmin mendicants and not thieves. So she called back the Brothers, made them sit and cooked with great attention some partly broken rice grains – all that she had. The two brothers collected two rolled banana leaves from inside a banana plant. They spread the leaves on the ground, sprinkled water on the leaves and waited for the food to arrive. The elderly Brahmin woman took a bronze bowl into the kitchen to get the cooked rice for the Brahmins.

What will she serve, her cooking pot had disappeared from the hearth! *These two men have been disowned by Lakshmi* – the Brahmin woman realized. She returned from her kitchen and came to the two Brothers, held them by their hands, and showed them out of the door. She rewarded them with her furor and consigned the Gods to the road. The Brothers became hopeless as they witnessed such conducts of the Brahmin woman; they moved on nevertheless and showed up in the lane of the Sufis.

Sufis were only part Hindus and did not offer cooked food to Brahmin mendicants. *These two are starving Brahmins* – so the Sufis realized and fetched for the mendicants five measures of popped rice.

Now Lakshmi, the lotus-faced Goddess knew of the episode with her insight. She summoned the Wind God right away and ordered forthwith: *Dear Wind God, make haste and blow away the popped rice of a few measures from the plates of the Brahmin brothers that they have received as alms.*

The Wind God raced bearing the summons of the Goddess. And up went the rice flakes in the wind as the Lords of the universe watched. *Do you hear, Jagannath?* Says Balaram, the Elder Brother, *when our life threatens to walk out of our bodies why consider the caste and roots of the donor? Let's go to the pond of lotuses; we can feed on the lotus tubers there and save our lives. We can also feast on the flowers and their piths; and if we get a lot of these edibles we can store the surplus.*

So contemplating the brothers moved; they entered the pond where lotuses of many petals blossomed. The lotus pond had waters of seven fathoms. Alas! Came a command from Goddess Lakshmi and the water turned to slush, of seven fathoms.

What do we do now? Says Jagannath, the Lord of the Universe; *there is no water in the pool and it is full of slush under the orders of Lakshmi, also known to be with a face of the lotus. How will we get here lotuses?*

The two Brother Gods proceeded further seeking food. The Gods trudged along. On the way they met a mendicant, a yogi who had no house or abode. Lord Jagannath said: 'O mendicant! We are hungry; do give us some rice from your plate.'

The eternally blissful mendicant looked at Lord Balaram and Lord Jagannath and said: 'You brothers have invited the curse of Lakshmi, the Goddess of Wealth. My mendicant's bowl was filled with fine rice cooked in milk. As soon as you asked me for a share the bowl was drained of the *kheer* I had collected. You will get nowhere, so it looks, either rice or water; therefore rush to the sea at once both you brothers. I had been to a house by the sea and the patron had given me *kheer*; my bowl was an extensive and endless buffet where you could eat and carry food home.'

Thus the truthful and the blessed directed the Brothers the way. *We'll surely go there,* the Brothers resolved and straightened their waists.

The lotus-faced, the prankster that she was, indulged in another of her pranks. She summoned the Sun God and fast decreed a pronouncement:

Hurry up and beam scorching rays,
the energy bestower,
on the sand and the ground that must sizzle
in your sweltering heat,
When the sand grains sizzle in the heat,
like the searing sand on which rice is roasted,
a lone step none must dare tread.

'Please Elder Brother,' speaks Lord Jagannath. 'I am unable to walk in this blazing sun. How are you able to run? I am at the end of my reason.'

Balaram hurried along as if he did not hear the words of his younger brother; he reached the portal – the Lion Gate of Lakshmi, the lotus-faced.

He entered the Lion Gate of the palace of Lakshmi, and called out for the Master of the House; his voice was loud and the housemaids surfaced with the noise.

One maid says to another:

I've never seen another destitute like this beggar at our door. There was one fatso like him who had once hounded our Goddess Lakshmi from the Great Temple.

The maid servants gossiped so and they gripped Balaram by the neck and shoved Him out to the road.

Lord Balaram returned thoroughly insulted and met his brother Lord Jagannath on the way. 'The maids shooed me away, Kanhai,' he grieved before his brother.

'What do we do now?' said the Lord of the Universe. 'How do we manage to survive? Let's go there again, Brother, and humble ourselves before the maids. *Give us some cooked rice:* let's say in our prayer.'

Then you must lead from the front, the Elder Brother announced, *you must beg the maids for cooked food and let me stand at your back and be your support.*

Thus the brothers went and arrived at the Lion Gate. They were baffled by the splendid temple that stood beyond the Lion Gate. 'Dear Jagannath,' said Balaram, 'now recite aloud hymns from Sama Veda with *pa* as the basic note.'

Lord Jagannath received the orders, and chanted Vedas beginning with a note set at *pa*. The cosmic expanse reverberated with the echoing incantations of the four Vedas: Rig, Yajur, Sama and Atharva.

Lakshmi was lounging on her four-poster when she heard the chanting of the hymns from Lord Jagannath. 'I have got deliverance,' she cried to herself, 'I've been redeemed of my transgression and the accumulated sins of a billion rebirths have washed away today.'

Then she said aloud: 'Go, maids, and find from the two brothers what it is that they want.'

The chief lady-in-waiting darted to the portal and asked: 'Dear Brahmins, feel free to say what you want? What are you begging for.'

Lord Jagannath looked at the chief lady-in-waiting and said: 'Can you give us a fistful of cooked rice?'

The waiting maids went to the inner quarters and rapidly narrated everything before Lakshmi.

When the Goddess heard the maids, she relented: I've earned this calumny myself, the lowly woman, I am at the root of this ridicule of the Great Brothers. I have caused such hardship for them. Then she said aloud to her maidservants: 'Go and ask the Brahmin brothers, how will they have cooked food from the kitchen of an untouchable woman? How will they take food in my house? Make it fast. Won't they shoulder the curse and calumny of having taken food from a *chandaal* woman, who has been ostracized from their society because of her lower caste? Moreover when I give them food from my house I have to touch the food. How can I pollute their food knowingly?'

The servant girls dispersed from near the Goddess and appeared before the Brahmins and narrated before them the discourse of Lakshmi. When He heard the words of the maids, the hungry Balaram said: 'Can you then give us new earthen cooking pots and utensils and raw ingredients? That will enable us to cook and eat food here.'

The servant girls carried the message before Lakshmi. The brothers themselves will cook their food and eat, said the girls.

The great Goddess was pleased to hear this. She

dispatched ten pots with the servant girls. She sent twenty quintals of raw rice grains. She sent the brothers a bunch of spinach, yam, tubers, plantains, aubergines. She also arranged for milk, yoghurt, cottage cheese, and sugar. *Now cook and eat as much as you want to* – she mumbled.

She retired indoors and contemplated: *if these two brothers cook and are able to feed themselves, will the men in the world ever require women in future?*

So the Goddess picked up a piece of firewood and chanted the hymns so that she could weaken the power of fire. 'Never blaze into fiery flames, Deity of Fire,' she said. 'So that neither the cooking pot on the hearth nor the water in it gets heated. How much so ever firewood they shove into the hearth, that must cinder away into ashes. The wood pieces must not flame, they must billow smoke.'

So spoke Lakshmi and thus was decreed her order. The Deity of Fire obeyed accordingly. All the firewood inside the hearth was reduced to embers. Yet the water in the pot did not warm a bit. Since Lotus-faced, the prankster was machinating her scheme, the cookware did not wear a line of stain on its bottom. The Goddess then dispatched her chambermaids to the brothers with fragrant massage oil. The maids asked: 'Dear Masters, is your food cooked or not? Use this oil for massage and have your bath fast.'

'The water does not heat up,' said Lord Jagannath. 'How can we cook? It's late now!'

'Listen dear,' says Balaram. Tell me quickly if the rice is cooked.'

'Do you hear Great Brother, the water is not even warm, how can the rice cook?'

Balaram says: 'Dear brother, you don't wash your face after waking up in the morning. Though you don't know the basics of cooking, yet you have taken on the role of the *Great Cook*. Move aside, and let me take over.'

So the elder Brahmin settled down to cooking. He blew into the hearth so that the firewood therein may blaze into flames, but it was to no avail. Balaram was so frustrated that he picked up a stick and smashed the cooking pot. The two brothers became miserable with hunger.

'What do we do now?' asked Balaram.

'I can't see a way out,' replied Jagannath, 'My body is wasting away in hunger.'

'Then listen to me, brother,' said Balaram. 'Let us opt to lose our caste and eat in her house. If we do not accept a few morsels of cooked rice from this house, death will come upon us Brothers.'

The chambermaid rushed indoors and conveyed the message to Lakshmi. The maid told the Goddess how the Brahmins broke their cooking pots and threw away the broken pieces. So Lakshmi brooded over the events: *How much the two Lords have suffered – the Lords who are known as Benefactors-of-the-poor!*

And then She, Lakshmi *Devi*, the Goddess, picked up a golden ladle and set off for the cooking quarters.

The Goddess cooked coarse brown rice,
roasted *moong* lentil cooked with gravy,
vegetables sweet and sour,
the sweet fragrant porridge of milk and fine rice,
a tangy dish of vegetables boiled in buttermilk,
spinach cooked with mustard and cumin powder;
sliced green plantains stir-fried in butter,
inner caulis of banana plant cooked
with several spices;
she cooked as much food as was offered

to the Lords in the temple everyday;
the coarse brown rice she cooked was a miracle.
The Mother prepared pancakes of rice powder
and homemade cheese dipped in thick milk;
and pancakes deep-fried in clarified butter,
dipped in cream saw her special care.
She cooked the items
as the Brahmins would relish them.
She cooked a curry of sweet tuber,
roasted sun-dried balls of black gram paste,
and spiced with cumin and poppy seeds paste.
She cooked a thousand items in as many pots
and placed the pots in appropriate order.
She prepared a drink of camphor, homemade cheese
and brown sugar made from palm juice,
and filled the potion into sixty huge pots.
She prepared a drink of tender coconut water
and dumplings of cottage cheese
with condiments of jaggery and crushed ginger roots.
How can I describe the culinary
expertise of the Mother?

She readied all these items in a few moments. She readied the plates with one dish of each item; for the dessert she kept the cake made of powdered rice and black grams, raisins, nuts, coconut gratings, wrapped in green banana leaves and roasted on burning charcoal.

Then the goddess told her maids: 'Go and give the Brahmins an oil massage so that they are ready for bath. Don't waver because they are Brahmins and you may pollute them. Don't hesitate because they are men. Because I *am* their slave.'

The maids were very happy with the turn of events and proceeded to meet the Brahmins. The maids said:

'Esteemed worshippers of Mother Cow! We will give you an oil massage and then you have a full bath.'

The Brothers relished the massage from the maids and bathed in fragrant water. They were given hand-made towels to wipe and robes of yellow silk to wear. The Brothers cleaned, and attired in new clothes, looked graceful, like Themselves.

'Brother Jagannath, why this honour suddenly?' asked Balaram. 'There is not a single man seen in this household. I think we will be executed – before a person is executed, he is given such sumptuous treatment. Let's flee from here immediately or else we shall lose our lives in a while from now.'

Lord Jagannath said: 'Now listen to me, Great Brother! Today you shall be the Lord of this household.'

'Dear younger brother, it is not proper on your part to talk like this.'

Lakshmi cleaned the whole palace
with her own hands.
She sprinkled the house
with camphor and oil of sandal wood.
She assembled for her guests utensils all made of gold:
platters, plates, quarter plates,
bowls and quarter-bowls.
She too arranged
basins for rinsing of the hands.
And tubs for washing the feet,
as is the practice with the Two Lords,
when they are offered the *bhog*.
She made and laid out
two sitting mats made of pure gold,
where the brothers will sit and have their food.
Then the Mother pleaded with her maids:

'Go and usher in my Lords,
dear ladies, and make it fast.'

The servant girls carried out the orders of the Goddess and appeared before the Brahmins. With humility, they entreated: 'Please O venerable Brahmins, do condescend to enter the palace as your humble dinner is ready.'

'Jagannath, you are a simpleton,' says Balaram. 'Lend me your ears. Here I can see only women. We do not see a single man in the entire palace. Would it be proper for us to enter the house? Go and fetch two banana leaves and let's eat here outside the palace.'

'Now listen to me Great Brother,' says Lord Jagannath. 'Today we shall be the masters of this home. Why are you so restless and insecure? The giver is giving away; must we forsake that?'

A petrified Balaram stayed put in his seat firmly and he had to be taken by the hand by his younger brother, the husband of Lakshmi. Balaram refused to be seated on the seat of gold set up for the banquet, and Jagannath forced him to take the seat of gold.

Lakshmi told her kitchen maid Tulasi, a Brahmin woman: 'Girl! The older Brahmin Balaram is the elder brother of my husband; how can I serve food to him? It is taboo for a woman to come too close to her husband's elder brother. Therefore I'll pass on the dishes from the kitchen through you. You must find out who is elder and who is younger. You must serve food to the elder brother first.'

The Brahmin woman swiftly carried the plates from the kitchen and asked the Brahmins: 'Which one of you is the older brother?'

'Have you become one-eyed?' asked Balaram. 'Can't you make out who is older? I am the elder brother.'

'Please do not be irate,' Tulasi said and served the first plate of rice before him.

She went back to the kitchen and returned with another plate of rice. When she returned with the plates, Balaram had already devoured the rice served to him in four mouthfuls and his plate was clean.

'Who took away all the rice from the plate of this Brahmin mendicant?' asked Tulasi.

'We have been starving for a long long time,' replied Balaram. 'So We gorged the contents instantly in four mouthfuls.'

An amused Tulasi stared at the brothers and said through her laughter: 'If you eat at this rate, you will starve and kill the family members of your host, O Brahmin mendicants! Don't you have sons and wives of yours that you wander from place to place just to have two meals a day?'

The housemaids brought in a thousand stacks of ripe banana. They brought in beverage made of nuts, cheese, sugar, fruits and milk in sixty vessels. The Gods were treated to delicacies in keeping with their taste, as Goddess Lakshmi sent over the food dishes one after another.

After the elaborate dinner, Balaram said: 'The food is delicious, like the food cooked by Goddess Lakshmi.'

'Can I ever find a wife like Lakshmi, Great Brother?' lamented Jagannath. 'You berated her and hounded her out of the Temple. She went off to the abode of her choice.'

Then the brothers were treated with *podapitha* – the cake made of rice and lentil paste, nuts and raisins and roasted over cinders wrapped in banana leaves.

'Great Brother Balaram,' Jagannath continued, 'Lakshmi knew my mind; she always served *podapitha* as the last dish of my meals.'

The brothers finished eating and performed the ritual of thanks-giving by sipping in some water from their cupped palms. Then they relished cones of betel leaves stuffed with nuts and spices, and ambled to the portal. Lakshmi was observing them out of her window.

She said to her maids: 'Dear girls, ask if the brothers are married.'

The maids rushed out and asked the Brahmins: 'Do you have sons and wives, Brahmins? Do you have homes of your own? Which country are you from? Where is your abode and what is your occupation?'

'Listen to me, O Ladies-in-waiting,' replied Jagannath. 'I have no possessions, no sprawling estates with orchards, and who will marry me? I have chased away a wife like Lakshmi from our household. We two brothers roam around like this bearing the misfortune and fate – a result of our karma – since the day we drove out Lakshmi.'

'Have you gone off your heads, O Brahmin mendicants?' countered the waiting maids. 'Does a man become poor if he forsakes his woman?'

'Do me a favour,' said Jagannath. 'What kind of wife harbingers ever-growing prosperity? What kind of wife causes the family to be annihilated without leaving a heir? What kind of woman deprives you of even a pot of stale gruel? Which kind of woman heralds in the good luck of beautiful attires and gold bracelets? What kind of ill-omened wife disintegrates the family? Do me a favour, go and ask these questions to the Lady of the House on our behalf.'

'Your garrulousness is unbecoming, O venerable mendicants!' replied the girls. 'You had been starving and were given a sumptuous meal. Now satiated, you want to parley with the lady of the house?'

'My brother is young,' interrupted Balaram. 'Please don't disclose any of his words before your house lady.'

'Why are you afraid, Brother?' asked Jagannath. 'Don't get worked up. After all, this is the house of Lakshmi. You need not worry at all.'

'Dear Jagannath, go near the Great Lakshmi,' said Balaram. 'Hold her hands and seek her forgiveness. Tell her that everything was our errancy. She can go anywhere she likes and we'll never object to that.'

With such orders from Brother Balaram Lord Jagannath rose with grace and set out for the inner quarters. He, the Yellow Robed Deity, sauntered along the corridors; and reached Lakshmi in the inner palace.

The Goddess came closer, in her hand sparkled a sprinkler, and a half-smile flickered on her face. She looked up at the Lord's countenance, and with enormous care and heedfulness and with the water from the sprinkler, she washed the feet of the Lord which are as beautiful as the lotus. She took a few drops of water dripping from the feet of the Lord, and smeared it on her forehead. A few more drops of it she sipped. With flowers of five hues she worshipped the lotus-feet of the Lord. Then she, Goddess Lakshmi, articulated looking her lord in the eye: 'You threw me out of my house, calling me a defiled woman - a *chandaaluni*. Now in the house of a *chandaaluni* you, the Lord of the Universe partook of food. Both you brothers have lost your caste, and have become polluted because you took food in the house of a defiled woman. Shame on your superciliousness and shame on your grandiloquence. May your pledges and promises be reduced to cinders, and shame, too, on your elder Brother.'

Maha Lakshmi, the great goddess reproached Lord

Jagannath for a long time. Lord Jagannath heard every word of it but remained silent.

Lakshmi, the weaver of great miracles, continued to chide: 'Now, dear Husband, tell me what brings you here.'

Jagannath remained pensive for a long time and then said:

'Give up your hubris O Mother of Creation.
You chide and reprimand us,
O the cohort of my life-force
without sufficient reason.
We plead before you to return to our Temple.
Though we are more powerful gods,
You vanquished our arrogance.
You assured that your glory shines on
through all the eons under the sun.
Because we forsook you
we endured agonizing suffering and pain.
The whole world learnt that
the two Brothers went begging for food.
The glorious account of your triumph
is now resounding in the universe:
that you gave us food,
and saved the lives of the famished gods.
Anyone listening on a Thursday
to this Holy Scripture,
will earn atonements for his sins of this life,
and the sins he has committed in lives before.
A woman who recites the verses
on the day dedicated to the worship of Lakshmi,
will be righteous in this life
and will find a place in heaven.
If a woman makes an oral exegesis
of this glorious Scripture,

who can ever measure the virtues
she earns for herself?'

Lord Jagannath ordained these proclamations and took her hands again.

But Goddess Lakshmi did not relent.

'First you must make a pledge O Lord of the Universe,'
She said.
'That the *chandaals* as well as the Brahmins
and people from all caste and class
shall feed each other inside the Temple.
After feeding each other
they shall not wash their smirched hands with water.
People from the highest caste and class
shall snatch food from
the fists of people from lowliest castes,
whose mere touch would
otherwise have defiled them.
After sharing the Holy Rice
No one will rinse his sloshy palms,
and instead,
everyone will clean his hand
by wiping it on the top of his head.
Inside the Temple everyone
must share the holy offerings
irrespective of the caste to which they are born.
Only when you concede to my stipulations
O Lord,
I shall enter Your holy abode.'

Jagannath, the-Lord-with-great-arms, solemnly agreed to the conditions imposed by Goddess Lakshmi and ordained: 'Let it be dear Lakshmi and let your magnificence shine through the eons.'

Parashar Speaks

Lord Jagannath ushered Lakshmi out of Her palace, holding Her by the hand, and set off for the Grand Temple to grace his abode. The temple glittered as if a hundred thousand moons shone to welcome the deities. Thus the Lord of the Universe set feet inside the Temple.

Indra, the God of rain and clouds supplicated: 'Glory be to my Lord! I pray for your kind attention.'

Brahma, the Father of the Creation implored: 'O Lord, do listen to the pending grievances of the world.'

When the Gods returned to their Grand Temple on earth, Gods in heaven celebrated. Varuna, the God of oceans and Kubera, the God of eternal wealth were performing as choreographers. The fairies - Rambha, Menaka, Chitralekha, Tulasi, Malati, Chanchala, Madalasi, Sushila and many others danced in happiness because Jagannath and Lakshmi had returned to the Temple.

Balaram said: 'Dear Jagannath, an abode retains its grandeur only in the presence of its goddess. When we two forlorn brothers trudged along the streets, people took us for burglars and dacoits and hounded us away. And I must confess, dear boy, that only now I realize how mighty Goddess Lakshmi is.'

Lakshmi entered her Temple. Jagannath entered the Great Temple. The retinue of waiting maids, Lady's maids, servant girls, chambermaids, ladies-in-waiting, housemaids and kitchen maids returned because Lakshmi had returned to the Grand Temple.

Jagannath, the Lord of the Universe, regained his happy-composure. The universe was in euphoria because the Lord spread his happiness all around.

"Dear Narada," says Parashar. "You have listened to this ancient and holy narration. Whose wrath forced the Lord of the Universe to go begging for foods? Whose benevolence saw a destitute woman to acquire immeasurable wealth and prosperity? She is Lakshmi and her munificence caused these miracles. If you read this Paean, you succeed everywhere in the world. All your sins and vices disappear just as darkness disappears with sunrise. Those who recite this Scripture, or lend their ears for its recitation, achieve the virtue of donating a hundred billion cows. This paean guides you along the path to salvation. Who has the competence to describe what all it will reward you with?"

Thus Speaks Balaram Das

So we come to the end of this Holy Narrative. Balaram Das, his soul inspired by divine bliss, has composed this paean in verse.

Black Eagle Books

www.blackeaglebooks.org
info@blackeaglebooks.org

Black Eagle Books, an independent publisher, was founded as a nonprofit organization in April, 2019. It is our mission to connect and engage the Indian diaspora and the world at large with the best of works of world literature published on a collaborative platform, with special emphasis on foregrounding Contemporary Classics and New Writing.